also by Christopher S. Wren

Hacks

The End of the Line: The Failure of Communism in the Soviet Union and China

Winners Got Scars Too: The Life and Legends of Johnny Cash

THE CAT WHO COVERED THE WORLD

The Adventures of Henrietta and Her Foreign Correspondent

CHRISTOPHER S. WREN

SIMON & SCHUSTER

New York London Toronto Sydney Singapore

SIMON & SCHUSTER
Rockefeller Center
1230 Avenue of the Americas
New York, NY 10020

Designed by Jeanette Olender
Manufactured in the United States of America

ISBN 0-684-87100-9

for Frances Braxton

Who enjoys nothing more than foreign adventure
. . . unless it's cats

"Would you tell me, please, which way I ought to go from here?"

"That depends a good deal on where you want to get to," said the Cat.

"I don't much care where—" said Alice.

"Then it doesn't matter which way you go," said the Cat.

"—so long as I get somewhere," Alice added as an explanation.

"Oh, you're sure to do that," said the Cat, "if you only walk long enough."

Lewis Carroll, *Alice's Adventures in Wonderland*

The Cat Who Covered the World

The Adventures of Henrietta and Her Foreign Correspondent

PRESS

Introduction

The most alluring adventuress I have known traveled the world in an elegant fur coat.

She savored life with all the brazen curiosity and spunky resourcefulness of, well, a foreign correspondent.

She flirted with customs officials and hung out with ambassadors.

She turned heads in airport lounges.

She became the talk of diplomatic dinners on four continents.

She developed a palate for caviar to rival the czar's.

Henrietta, as this exquisite creature was named, did not lack for admirers who yearned to caress her. But she could take care of herself, though willfulness led her almost fatally astray in the Middle East.

As our mutual wariness turned to love, Henrietta came to share my bed. And my own long-suffering wife never complained.

Of course, our family cat—did I neglect to mention that Henrietta was a cat?—wasn't given any choice about embarking on so glamorous a career.

But far better than most tourists, she adjusted to jet lag, bizarre food, exotic languages, and forbidding climates. And just in case of trouble, she kept her claws sharpened on the furniture at five foreign bureaus of *The New York Times.*

Like any good journalist, she was even blessed with a sturdy bladder.

Henrietta matured into the intrepid sort of companion

you'd want to hit the road with. It was why a curmudgeon about cats like me grew so fond of my fellow traveler in the many thousands of miles that we logged together through Europe, Asia, and Africa, as well as North America.

For Henrietta's adventures as I recount them here actually happened.

In reconstructing the details of Henrietta's remarkable odyssey, I am indebted to the memories and invaluable contributions of my wife, Jaqueline, and our children, Celia and Chris, who tended to invest more time and patience in our cat than I did.

I must also thank my *Times* colleagues from A to Z—or at least from Glenn Collins to Joyce Wadler—for encouraging me to share Henrietta's story with a larger audience.

How often they would pause from their own fine writing to say, "Yeah, your cat sounds great, but I'm on this tight deadline that you wouldn't believe, in fact the damn piece was due five minutes ago, so can't your cat's exploits be put in a book that I'll promise to read when I'm no longer up to my ears in alligators and find time to get a life?"

I have taken some liberties only with the dialogue of the conversations that occurred in the course of Henrietta's travels, if not in the precise language quoted here, then very much in the same context and spirit.

In the lands through which she traveled, our cat found herself called *koshka* by Russians, *il gatto* by Italians, *kissa* by Finns, *quttah* by Egyptians, *le chat* by French (and Quebecois), *neko* by Japanese, *mao* by Chinese, *a gata* by Portuguese, *die kat* by Afrikaners (and Dutch), and *ikati* by Zulus.

Naturally, all of them were talking about Henrietta.

Our cat did more than dispel the bedlam that all too often characterizes the life of a foreign correspondent's family overseas. Through a succession of postings in Moscow, Cairo, Beijing, Ottawa, and Johannesburg, and during other, shorter visits to Rome, Paris, Lisbon, and Tokyo, she came to provide the continuity of hearth and home.

If Henrietta was there, our children decided, so was home.

New York

The cat arrived with a bottle of Scotch.

The marketing pitch struck me as a bit obvious when I came across the offer on a bulletin board at *Newsweek* magazine, where I was employed at the time as a general editor to write every week on the subject of national affairs.

One of the magazine's researchers had posted the offer, explaining that her cat had given birth to a litter of kittens that required the usual loving homes. Her small apartment, she lamented, had room for only one cat.

Well, any journalist with ambitions of living off wars, coups, earthquakes, and other disasters would be callow indeed not to snicker at the dilemma of too many cats in a New York City apartment. So the appeal had little impact until I got to the last line, which grabbed my attention. This lady evidently knew her target audience:

"A bottle of Scotch comes with every kitten!"

I don't drink Scotch, though my wife, Jaqueline, has been known to consume as much as a thimbleful over the course of a year. But enough journalists do drink Scotch that we never seemed to have any left after our friends visited.

I hadn't found time to find an engaging Christmas present for our two children, Celia and Chris, who were then about six and two and a half years old. They were still in mourning for a previous cat that had trotted off one day from our weekend cottage and was absentminded enough not to return, which had only confirmed my prejudices about the fickleness of felines.

It embarrasses me to admit that I breathed a sigh of relief at the loss. I had no interest in replacing the cat who had gone missing in action. But when I answered the note, my colleague at *Newsweek* actually made her cat's litter sound intriguing.

The kittens' mother was a pedigreed Siamese, I learned, who through a careless encounter had found herself in the family way. The particulars were sketchier about their father, a hit-and-run Lothario of indeterminate origin in the borough of Queens.

The outcome was that on Christmas Day, the donor showed up at our apartment on Manhattan's Upper West Side bearing the kind of cardboard box ordinarily associated with supermarkets. Jaqueline had just taken Celia and Chris out to see her parents in Scarsdale, a suburb of New York City. I was under instructions to appear in time for holiday dinner bearing their surprise present, a brand-new kitten.

"Merry Christmas," said my *Newsweek* colleague, which did not surprise me because she was a thoroughly nice lady. She thrust the box at me.

It looked empty except for the soiled newspaper pages that lined the box. Then, in one corner, I saw a ball of gray fluff not much larger than what sometimes accumulated in our clothes dryer.

Gingerly, I scooped up the fluff. It wriggled in my hands. A tiny tongue licked my finger, probing for a mother's teat. I have to concede that I was touched. There was something so ephemeral and vulnerable about this young thing that I failed to see how it could survive without its mother, and I was no fit surrogate father. What should you feed a creature that hardly fills your outstretched hand?

"That's it?" I asked. "Is it old enough?"

"More than a month," the donor told me.

This didn't look possible. Still, the gift had to be considered from a larger perspective.

"And the Scotch?" I prompted helpfully. We did have a deal here.

"Of course," my *Newsweek* colleague said, "the Scotch."

She rummaged through a large paper bag and handed over a generous bottle of Johnnie Walker Red Label.

"Merry Christmas," she said again and withdrew to the elevator before I could hand back box and bottle. She had more kittens to distribute.

I set the carton on the kitchen floor beside the washing machine and went to the refrigerator to find some milk. I poured the milk into a saucer, which is the kind of thing you do for a kitten when you can't think of something better, and set it down next to the gray fluff. It seemed too small to call a real kitten, though now I could discern a head and wispy tail.

The kitten headed not for the milk but under a pile of dirty laundry that I had promised Jaqueline I would toss into the washing machine.

I peeled away the underwear, socks, and towels, making sure, when I deposited each item into the washing machine, that a kitten was not attached. Feeding the children's Christmas present into the spin cycle would be hard to explain.

Finally, there was only one shirt left. I picked it up, and nothing was under it. I was prepared to sift through the contents of the washing machine again until I saw the gray fluff, this time wafting across the kitchen linoleum. I snatched it up before it could disappear under the refrigerator.

The kitten had a fast set of paws, not to mention a mind of its own.

Gotcha, I exulted. I popped it back into the box and this time added the saucer of milk. I fetched my overcoat and found the car keys.

"Let's go meet the rest of your family," I told it. I had better things to think about, like a job offer from *The New York Times.*

It's become a cliché for people writing books about cats to purport that they didn't like them until they acquired one. I wish I had patented that cliché, or at least elevated it to the proprietary level of an Internet Web site: catchurl.com.

I'd always considered myself a dog kind of person, prepared to assume the burden of command that a dog expects of you as leader of the pack. When you say, "Hey, little guy, let's go out and shag some flies, and then we'll come back and pop open a couple of cold brews and catch the Mets on the tube," the dog will start wagging its tail and slobbering before you have finished, because it knows exactly what you're talking about, which is more than your spouse probably does. Not only does the dog let you know what really cool ideas you come up with, but it will rush to beat you out the door.

Try bouncing that same conversation off a cat. Its contemptuous stare will remind you that you never got around to cleaning its litter box, or emptying the dishwasher, and—the look will ask—how can you think about goofing off when you haven't started doing your income tax?

No, cats couldn't care less about being your buddy and chasing balls. They inhabit an aloofness I always took for reproach or ingratitude.

Put my skepticism down to the fortunes of a privileged childhood in Hollywood, California, in a family that lacked for nothing but financial security, which is to say money. My parents were both actors, immensely talented ones who like so many in the performing arts were sometimes hard put to cover the rent at the end of the month. It did not help that they loaned what they had to other actors in more dire straits and, so far as I can recall, were never paid back. We weren't poor, but we were sometimes broke.

Our compensation was being entertained by actors who kept dropping by our home in Hollywood because they could smell my mother's homemade chicken and noodles from the far end of Sunset Boulevard and would stay around and talk well into the night. When I eavesdropped with my twin sister, Ginny, on their lively conversations in our living room, the adults were arguing not about the stock market or real estate—they couldn't afford either—but about whether Shakespeare's creativity had been enhanced by having a theater at hand to stage whatever he wanted to write.

Who needed a dog or a cat when our home abounded with actors with the talent to amuse us at the slightest pretext?

Our parents, who desperately wanted to give us a normal childhood, did once get us a kitten, but it died after bestowing a dose of ringworm on my sister. Then the family doctor diagnosed my running sniffles as symptoms of an allergy to cats.

Our father bought an Irish setter, which promptly broke its leg and had to be put to sleep. We went through a couple of cocker spaniels that were given away when our parents' search for work shuttled us between Hollywood and New York.

It was a lesson best learned early: pets became pests if you were in an occupation that kept you in perpetual motion.

Celia and Christopher were so enchanted with their new kitten that they called her Henrietta, after a puppet on their favorite television show, *Mister Rogers' Neighborhood*. Well, that's not entirely true. They had actually named her Henrietta

Meow Meow Pussycat Wren, which makes me gag even as I write it down. I had proposed something more generic petwise, like Fido, but stylishly spelled P-h-y-d-e-a-u-x.

Once she grew into the graceful proportions of a proper cat, she became simply Henrietta. Her fur was shaded a definite gray, but with brindled hints of brown and the faintest tiger striping down her back and sides. She looked noble in profile, having inherited the trim Siamese features of her mother. She was petite, from her dainty nose and whiskers down to an elegant tail. Even fully grown, Henrietta never weighed much more than eight pounds.

By now I was working as a reporter for *The New York Times,* because I had always wanted to become a foreign correspondent. While *Newsweek* kept promising to think about it, Seymour Topping, the editor who had brought me to the *Times,* had been one of the legendary China correspondents and treated my wish as inevitable, though not imminent. The notion of traveling about the world satisfying your curiosity, seeing the Kremlin and the Pyramids and the Great Wall of China, and doing it on an expense account sounded like a dream job. And it came with a regular paycheck. Learning new languages posed no problem. My parents used to bring home fat scripts and digest them overnight, so rote memorization struck Ginny and me as no more unusual than doing our math homework for school at one sitting.

The *Times* hired me in part because I had studied Russian at Dartmouth, so I hoped to be considered when something opened up at the Moscow bureau in a few years. That left me plenty of time to dispose of Henrietta, who I hoped might follow the example of her predecessor and run away by the time the post opened.

In the meantime, I was put to work covering New York

City, mostly welfare scams, homicides, and assorted mayhem du jour. The assignment I remember most vividly involved the city's oldest homicide victim, or so the assignment editor told me that night. I rushed down to a tenement on Manhattan's Lower East Side and interviewed the victim's grieving son while the cops combed the shabby walk-up apartment for clues to her killer. With my deadline looming, I called in from a pay phone on the street outside to dictate a summary of my story in a cold drizzle.

"The victim, who was seventy-seven years old—," I was saying when the editor on the other end of the line broke in.

"Ninety-one years old," he said, contradicting my account. "The police report said she was ninety-one."

"Her son insists she was seventy-seven," I demurred. "We did the math, in Spanish."

There was a short pause. "Hell, that's no story," the assignment editor said, and ordered me back to the newsroom.

The *Times* and I have both come a long way since then.

Six months after I joined the newspaper, one of its two Moscow correspondents suddenly asked to return home for family reasons, well ahead of schedule. The editors looked around the newsroom for someone who spoke Russian, and saw me. Would I be at all interested?

Responding to this unanticipated miracle must have taken me all of three seconds. Once the shock subsided, I replied as calmly as I could, "How soon can I leave?"

The biggest problem I foresaw was our cat, Henrietta, because I didn't know how she would survive in strange new surroundings. She was playful enough with Celia and Chris. In fact, they had grown devoted to her.

But our cat had no visible street smarts. Her only travels

outside our apartment had been in the backseat of our car to the cottage we rented in Putnam County, a couple of hours north of our Manhattan apartment. Even there, Jaqueline hesitated to let her out for fear of the local dogs or wilder predators, whom we suspected of having done in our previous cat.

One Saturday afternoon, Henrietta decided to climb a tree, and we spent the rest of the weekend coaxing her down.

"Don't be afraid," Jaqueline told the cat. "We'll catch you if you fall."

As a gesture of confidence, my soul mate added, "If Daddy misses, I'll drive you to the hospital."

Henrietta, pointed up but looking down, lost her grip and fell. Her claws deployed into my skull and shoulders. I pried her off and deposited her on the ground. She promptly dashed off and hid for a very long time under the porch, unhurt but definitely shaken.

In describing Henrietta back then, "spunky" and "intrepid" are not the sort of words that spring to mind. Her clumsy fall out of an uncomplicated tree did not augur well for a life behind the Iron Curtain.

It should be apparent by now that Henrietta and I didn't think much of each other, not at first. Henrietta sensed my fear that keeping her around would make it harder for me to succeed as a foreign correspondent.

To begin with, the cat would have to be given all kinds of expensive inoculations against rabies and more exotic diseases. She would need a traveling case heavy enough to withstand the tons of boxes and bags dumped on her by the baggage handlers. And for all its corporate benevolence, the *Times* refused to subsidize cats for its correspondents, so we would have to invest a tidy sum in Henrietta's travels.

Not least, I wondered whether my editors would consider

it frivolous for a new reporter to venture onto the vast, windswept Russian steppes with cat in tow.

I invented all sorts of reasons for leaving Henrietta behind, as much for her sake as ours. I reminded Jaqueline that pets couldn't just rove hither and yon; many countries impose quarantine restrictions that our cat would not enjoy and might not survive. Another reporter I knew had to turn down a coveted assignment to our London bureau after his wife refused to submit their dog to the mandatory six-month quarantine in Britain; shortly thereafter, he quit the *Times.*

Over dinner one evening, I summoned up the courage to explain our dilemma to Chris and Celia, who by now had attained the prime listening ages of three and nearly seven years old.

Very soon we would be moving to a fairy-tale land called Russia, far, far away. And didn't Celia and Chris agree with me that Henrietta would be ever so much happier staying behind in New York City, where she had ever so many relatives?

And no—I anticipated the children's first question—taking all her relatives with us to Russia wasn't an option, because Henrietta couldn't tell us who they were or where they lived.

As the debate unfolded around our kitchen table, my mind was struggling to compile a short list of acquaintances who might consider taking the cat off our hands for two bottles of Scotch, or three at most.

Chris was not too young to sense that something here was amiss. "But what about Henrietta?" he inquired suspiciously. Until now, he had let Celia do most of the talking.

I started to explain that our cat would have much more fun remaining in New York, but somewhere lovely and spacious, of course, maybe even Central Park. Then Celia interrupted me.

"Henrietta's going too," Celia assured her little brother.

"I'm not sure that's such a good—" I began.

Celia now addressed the cat in question, who at the time was more curious about what we were eating for dinner that she hadn't been allowed to sample first.

"Henrietta," Celia said, "you're going to live in Russia, aren't you?"

Henrietta perked up her ears at the prospect of foreign adventure.

Chris, beaming with relief, looked to his mother for reassurance. "Henrietta's going too?"

"How could we go anywhere without Henrietta?" Jaqueline assured our little boy. "Why, she'll even be riding right in the plane with us."

"I'll hold her all the way," Chris volunteered.

"We'll take turns," Celia said firmly.

The heart trumps the head every time. Henrietta went abroad because Celia and Chris could not conceive of living anywhere without her.

So the family cat who couldn't even find her way down from a tree was headed straight for the malevolent heart of the Evil Empire, as Ronald Reagan later described the Soviet Union. And Henrietta didn't choose her fate; I did.

If I recall correctly, the relationship between the human and feline species of fauna in our diverse world developed many thousands of years ago, when woman and man began to till their crops and store the bounty of the harvests. Cats, as natural predators, were attracted to the rats and mice that in turn were attracted to the stored grain.

So a compact evolved without benefit of lawyers. The party of the first part, i.e., the cat, would consent to cohabit with the parties of the second part, i.e., woman and man, and keep the rodent population to a minimum in return for a cozy place by the fire, timely petting, and other such creature comforts as both sides deemed reasonable and proper.

This primal compact never stipulated being jabbed with a vaccination needle, locked inside a cramped box, stuffed into the bowels of a whining jetliner, and flown halfway around the world to a Communist dictatorship that had not met a harvest it couldn't screw up.

But when did we ever hesitate to inconvenience the other creatures who share our earth?

During my army service, it was popular for a mercifully short time to adopt an animal as an involuntary mascot, who would get decked out in a makeshift parachute and dropped twelve hundred feet from an aircraft in flight along with the paratroopers, who were paid an extra $55 a month ($110 for us lieutenants) for voluntarily risking their lives. The displays of airborne bravado offered no such jump pay or other perks for the animals involved.

I heard of one terrified monkey that had climbed the risers of its parachute, spilling out all the air and reaching terminal velocity before it hit the ground.

The tale of a bear cub ended more satisfactorily. The battalion involved had not jumped for some months, and when it did, the cub, which had now grown into bearhood, balked at exiting the aircraft when the light flashed green. The bear took a more sensible route and turned on the soldiers hooked up to follow it out the door. The jump was aborted, and the bear was dishonorably discharged from mascot duty.

Such stories may be apocryphal, but I doubt it, recalling the silly things we had to do to earn our parachute wings. I was scared every time I jumped, so I could well imagine how an animal would feel if it were chucked out of a plane moving at a velocity in excess of 125 miles an hour.

I can claim credible secondhand knowledge of Oscar, a white mouse that *Life* magazine once hailed as the world's tiniest paratrooper. The *Life* article featured photographs of wee Oscar peering timidly out from the parachute harness of his handler, a tough Green Beret in the Tenth Special Forces Group and, after being detached in midair, floating gracefully toward earth at Bad Tolz, Germany, buoyed by a parachute that looked a lot like a cotton handkerchief.

Later I met a sergeant from the Tenth who had just been reassigned to the Seventh Special Forces Group, the unit in which I was finishing my military service. Out of curiosity, I inquired how many jumps the world's tiniest paratrooper had actually logged.

The sergeant chuckled at the memory. "All the cats in Bad Tolz deployed on that drop zone," he said.

How, then, I asked, could a parachuting mouse manage to escape and evade so many cats and jump again?

The sergeant stared as though I'd landed on my head twice too often.

"We changed mice," he said.

Moscow

On an icy New Year's Eve, our cat, looking small and very frightened, flew from London into Moscow's Sheremetyevo International Airport, accompanying the foreign correspondent who didn't want her and his wife and two children who refused to leave the United States without her.

Entering the Soviet Union, we confronted a potentially serious problem: on New Year's Day, *The New York Times* would begin publishing excerpts from Aleksandr Solzhenitsyn's *The Gulag Archipelago.* My editors feared that once Solzhenitsyn's exposé of the Soviet penal system appeared, the Kremlin could retaliate by refusing to let me into the country. But if I was already sitting in the *Times's* Moscow bureau, the authorities would hesitate to throw me out, knowing that the American government would respond by expelling a Russian correspondent from Washington.

I worried that Henrietta would delay our arrival. To sneak in as inconspicuously as possible—my incognito entourage included only a beautiful wife, two lively, towheaded, English-speaking children, a couple of dozen pieces of luggage, and the family cat—we had chosen New Year's Eve, a holiday on which Russians are traditionally preoccupied with debauching themselves into collective oblivion.

The biting winter cold sent Henrietta into shivers as her travel cage was trundled past snowdrifts bordering the slick tarmac. Sheremetyevo's arrivals terminal reeked of wet woolen overcoats, chlorine disinfectant, coarse cigarettes, and other pungent odors. They warned her that this destination was neither familiar nor hospitable.

Suspicious border guards with bayonets fixed on their Kalashnikov assault rifles scrutinized the stream of passengers as we milled past. The customs officials watched Henrietta's travel cage being dumped on the grimy inspection counter. They resented having to work on New Year's Eve, which more fortunate Russians were celebrating with sentimental toasts, passionate gropings, and torrents of vodka.

A gray-jacketed customs officer looked us over and then saw the cat cage.

"Skoro budyet," he said. It will happen soon.

"What will be soon?" I asked.

"You brought an animal with you," he said. "The veterinary inspection will happen soon."

"Soon" turned out to be more than a half hour until the veterinarian on duty finally showed up. She was a stout woman wearing a long white lab coat and exhibiting the surliness of the Soviet bureaucracy. It was up to her to decide whether the trembling contents of Henrietta's cage deserved admittance to the Union of Soviet Socialist Republics or should be packed off to some quarantine confines with all the comforts of a Siberian salt mine.

The veterinarian frowned at the untranslated English of the cat's vaccination papers, which she obviously could not read. A *nyet* from her would leave us mired in the Soviet bureaucracy long after our window of opportunity had passed. I started to panic.

But as I silently reproached myself for putting my job in jeopardy by dragging a cat to my first foreign assignment, the vet pulled Henrietta out of her cage, but gently, and her official brusqueness melted away.

"Kakaya krasivaya Amerikanskaya koshka!" marveled the veterinarian. What a beautiful little American cat!

An American cat? The rest of attendant Soviet officialdom jostled in for a look. Peering up, Henrietta greeted them with a plaintive meow that seemed to plead, Will you get me out of here?

Laughter replaced the sullen silence as the officials took turns petting the American cat—yes, my Henrietta.

"Koshka ustala." The cat must be tired traveling all the way from America, someone observed. In fact, we had stopped over in London, where Henrietta had had to spend a couple of nights in the quarantine facility near London's Heathrow International Airport. More likely, she desperately needed to find a litter box.

And the yawning American children, someone else said. *"Malyshi ustali tozhe."* The kids look tired, too.

For Henrietta's sake we were rushed through the remaining formalities faster than I've ever cleared a Russian airport on scores of flights. No longer was anyone concerned about how much money we were carrying or what kind of subversive literature we might have stashed in the linings of our suitcases. Whatever ideological distaste the Russian officials were obliged to display toward decadent Americans exempted Henrietta, a cat who would look at home on any Russian hearth.

Far from slowing us up, Henrietta had interceded to get us into the country. We were asleep, with the cat curled up on one of the children's beds in our new apartment overlooking Moscow's Ring Road, by the time Solzhenitsyn's denunciation of the country that had just admitted us appeared on the *Times*'s front page.

35

The Russians have a tradition, or call it a superstition, that when you take possession of a new home, your cat should enter first to become acquainted with the *domovoi,* a kind of spirit inhabiting the house, somewhat like a hobgoblin or leprechaun but less intrusively quaint. It is up to the cat to befriend the spirit and make your stay more pleasant. We must have followed that sequence when we arrived from Sheremetyevo airport, though we weren't aware of the custom yet, because our immediate concern after completing a trip with Henrietta was to free her from the confines of her box as soon as possible.

I never actually met the *domovoi* living in our apartment at 12/24 Sadovo-Samotechnaya, though I imagined him to be a tiny wizened Cossack wearing a jaunty *shapka,* or fur hat, and stomping about in felt boots. But Henrietta evidently hit it off with him, because the cramped Moscow apartment came to feel like home for the next four years.

Having a *domovoi* wasn't scary and could even be useful, because whenever you lost or misplaced something, such as your passport or car keys, you left the house spirit a piece of candy in a corner of the kitchen and the missing item was bound to turn up, or so some of our Russian friends insisted. The candy wouldn't actually be consumed by the *domovoi*—it was the gesture that mattered—so you had to remember to throw it out before the mice—or the cat—got it.

From my *Times* predecessor, we inherited the five-room apartment on the ground floor of 12/24 Sadovo-Samotechnaya, a solid if shabby-looking building constructed by German prisoners of war during the final months of World War II. We lived longer in that apartment than anywhere else in my years as a foreign correspondent.

The courtyard of "SadSam," as its Western residents nicknamed our building, was bounded on one side by an L-shaped building with three separate entrances and on the other by a high yellow wall. Our apartment was in the east wing. The *Times's* Moscow bureau was on the third floor of the west wing, so it took only a few minutes for Henrietta to trot over and visit me, including her ascent of two flights of worn stairs. There was the usual Russian elevator, which Henrietta and the rest of us avoided using whenever possible because, like other Soviet-era elevators, it was used to going on strike between floors.

The only entrance from the street passed through a gate patrolled twenty-four hours a day by gray-uniformed sentinels from the Committee for State Security, better known by its Russian initials, KGB. The guards were there to keep out ordinary Russians and to phone in our movements to some central switchboard whenever we left the compound. But they showed no interest in tracking our cat.

Were I as poor a judge of news as I am of cats, I would have had to quit journalism long ago. Contrary to my expectation that Henrietta would be too timid to leave her new apartment in Moscow, the cat's first instinct was to satisfy an intense curiosity about her new surroundings.

We can only guess at what went through Henrietta's mind when she set out to inspect her new neighborhood. "The soul of another is darkness . . .," wrote the Russian writer Anton Chekhov (1860–1904), borrowing word for word from a Russian proverb, *"Chuzhaya dusha potemki."* Or maybe the proverb was borrowed from Chekhov, because Russians are fond of quoting from their pantheon of great writers and poets.

But Chekhov was definitely referring here to the likes of Henrietta, for he added, ". . . and a cat's soul more than most."

He had in mind a kitten that had enraged his uncle Pyotr Demyanich by fleeing at the sight of a mouse in the kitchen.

"Unacquainted with real life, having no store of accumulated impressions, his mental processes could only be instinctive," Chekhov had assumed of the kitten earlier, "and he could only picture life in accordance with conceptions that he had inherited, together with his flesh and blood, from his ancestors, the tigers" in Darwinian fashion.

Henrietta would have thrilled cranky old Uncle Pyotr. Her atavistic instinct kicked in whenever she ventured into the old streets of northern Moscow's Bauminsky district. She reverted to her innate sense of smell and hunting instincts as naturally as a kitten first probes for signs of life beyond the warm security of its mother's litter.

It took just a few days for Henrietta to teach herself to exit our ground-floor kitchen by springing up on the table and scrambling out to the courtyard through her own private door. It was called the *fortechka,* a cat-sized ventilation pane set into the double-paned windows in Russia and usually left open for welcome fresh air on all but the coldest winter days.

Henrietta left dainty pawprints in the snow as she trotted past the KGB post. Sometimes the guards were busy with our son, Chris, who had brought a large stash of chewing gum from the United States and would trade some of it with our KGB sentries for tiny red-enameled Soviet badges, called *znachki,* and an occasional lesson in throwing snowballs.

The first stop on Henrietta's daily rounds was invariably the tall steel crane blocking off Yermolaya Street. A testimonial to the fervor of Soviet construction, the crane stood idle when we arrived and was still unused when we left Moscow four years later. Any newcomer to Moscow in those days marveled that so many cranes dominated the skyline, taking them for a sign of progress when in fact nothing of the sort was happening.

It did not take long for Henrietta to see through this Bolshevik *disinformatsiya,* which she astutely commented upon by pausing to tinkle in the snowdrift that was hardening against the crane's rusting foundations.

Henrietta continued south down Yermolaya Street, past our fragrant local bakery to the garbage cans sitting outside the Lebanese Embassy and a few other diplomatic missions. Here she engaged in a bit of scavenging before the KGB garbage truck arrived to cart away the diplomatic trash and sift through it for potential classified material.

Our Moscow neighbors took no notice of Henrietta because she looked pretty much like any local cat out on the town. In fact, Russian cats tend to look bushier because they are longer-haired than American cats. But as another proverb cited by Rita Polyakova, the Russian-born wife of my *Times* colleague David Stout, observes, "All cats are gray at night."

After a while, Henrietta turned eastward, meandering through back alleys to Tsentralny Rynok, or the informal Central Market. She hung about the cavernous shed cadging bits of fish and cabbage from collective farmers who had carted in produce raised on their private plots. Here tomatoes, potatoes, radishes, carrots, and cabbage, far more succulent than what you'd find in the state stores, were displayed by peasant women on the wooden counters like precious gems exhibited on a jeweler's black cloth.

It was at the Central Market that Henrietta was first introduced to vegetables. I know that cats are carnivores accustomed to eating meat and fish. I'm not suggesting that our cat was the sort to pass up a prime sirloin for the vegetarian special, arugula and all. But vegetables, cooked with fish or meat and a little rice, came to constitute part of her diet. I would love to set up a chain of gourmet pet-food shops called Henrietta's Secret, where cat lovers could choose from a nourishing range of exotic edibles, and not-so-edibles, that sustained our cat during her years abroad.

I monitored Henrietta's activities in Moscow when I caught sight of her from the window over my desk in the *Times* bureau. Or going out to drive the bureau car to an interview, I'd watch her sitting and staring at a potential mouse hole in some wall down the street, or maybe stalking the occasional bird. Or a neighbor in our compound would call out, "Say, wasn't that your cat I saw down at the Uzbekistan Restaurant? Don't you feed her enough?"

I had assumed that our cat was pretty much useless beyond its entertainment value for Celia and Chris. It did not take long for Henrietta to prove me wrong.

One evening, I came home from the *Times* bureau for dinner to find Jaqueline in an agitated state. "You've got to do something about Henrietta," she said.

I was tempted to say, "I'll book her on the next Aeroflot flight back to New York." But I held my tongue. My wife led me into the living room, where we encountered Henrietta suspended halfway to the ceiling like some levitating swami.

To be more accurate, the cat had clawed her way up the bright curtains and was dangling inches below a *mysha*—a small Russian mouse—whose palpable fear had overcome the natural forces of gravity. Before I could step in, Henrietta lunged upward to seize the mouse's tail in her teeth, executed an incredible back flip in midair, and landed four-footed on the carpet with her wriggling prey.

I was dazzled. Our clumsy New York kitten had just demonstrated her dexterity at a skill that would make her indispensible to our years abroad. And if the denouement of the chase turned somewhat bloody, well, Lenin had warned us that a cat wearing gloves catches no mice. Or was that Benjamin Franklin?

In the United States at least, no expense is spared in treating cats as ornamental and amusing. But they get fewer and fewer opportunities to be useful in the ways that they have been since the dawn of civilization. Our Henrietta was happy to earn her keep by harvesting mice, a chore that American cats are seldom called upon to perform.

I'm no longer awestruck when people tell me what cute tricks their cat has been taught, because there isn't that much worthwhile you can teach a cat that it doesn't already know. It would be helpful if your cat learned to program the videocassette recorder or could surf the Internet or sort out the intricacies of hedge funds in the world of high finance, especially if it earned enough to cover the cost of niblets and litter.

But the primal compact only requires cats to earn their keep by exterminating mice, and it amazes me how well they continue to keep their side of the bargain when given half a chance.

And for Henrietta our apartment building in Moscow was a cat's paradise because it abounded in rodents, thanks largely to the old garbage chute outside our kitchen. The building's eight stories' worth of trash splattered down into dirty metal bins in the basement. The bins were carted off, I'm told, to a recycling center where KGB gnomes recycled the contents, sorting through the containers for telltale scraps of paper that might reveal what nefarious plots the building's residents, all foreign diplomats and journalists, were hatching against the Kremlin.

In the four years that we lived at 12/24 Sadovo-Samotechnaya, I cannot recall that the chute was ever cleaned of the crusty, oozing accumulation of rotting borscht and other garbage. This meant that our cat never lacked for opportunities to track down and eviscerate whatever rodents had infiltrated the premises.

Occasionally, I carried Henrietta over to the *Times* news bureau at the other end of the courtyard and put her to work sniffing for mice around the holes and cracks in the office walls, like a city inspector tracing a gas leak.

Confronted with limitless opportunities to hone her skills, Henrietta became a diligent mouser. Once, when Jaqueline intervened to rescue a mouse and tossed it outside, Henrietta wailed the night away at the loss of her prize.

She enjoyed the chase as much as the capture, though her hunting prowess proved something of an embarrassment one evening when we hosted an elegant diplomatic dinner party for wall-to-wall ambassadors who had squeezed into our snug apartment.

Our guest of honor, the ambassador of Pakistan, was chatting with the ambassador of Tunisia about some nuance of Soviet policy in the Middle East, while I eavesdropped for any morsel of information that might justify an article.

From the corner of my eye, I saw Henrietta triumphantly trotting into the living room. A mouse, somewhat larger than Henrietta's usual catches, dangled from her clamped jaws.

Their assembled excellencies paused in midconversation and stared down. So did everyone else in the room. Silence fell. I looked at Jaqueline, who was equally chagrined, for some signal as to how we would get Henrietta out of there.

Fortunately, the ambassador of Pakistan was nothing if not a consummate diplomat. A gentleman of elegance, he did not recoil.

"What a clever cat you must be!" he graciously complimented Henrietta. "You want to show us the mouse you have caught."

He patted her and resumed his conversation with the Tunisian ambassador, diplomatically ignoring the dying rodent that Henrietta had dropped beside his polished black shoe.

There was a round of nervous applause for Henrietta's catch, though more than a few of our guests were looking about for higher ground in case the cat, motivated by the Pakistani ambassador's compliment, returned with more trophies to present.

I murmured apologies all around and, rather than desert the party to rummage for a whisk broom and dustpan, hoisted the defunct mouse by the tail and removed it as delicately as I could to the kitchen's garbage chute. Henrietta followed me, unable to understand what all the fuss was about.

Beyond competing for her share of leftovers at the Central Market, Henrietta did not hang about with local Russian cats. Small though she was, she was never reticent about defending her new turf. You can take the cat out of New York City, but you can't take New York City out of the cat.

I never saw her actually get into a fight until after we left Moscow. But the shaggier Russian cats tended to stay clear of her, the sole exception being our neighborhood nemesis, Rasputin. He was a disheveled black tomcat who had been adopted by a disheveled French correspondent.

I would love to tell you about Henrietta's passionate romance with Rasputin. But the fact is, we had had her spayed before leaving New York, which simplified things all around. Rasputin wouldn't have been an appropriate swain in any case, because she had better taste. Henrietta's initial curiosity about the Russian tomcat developed into an unmitigated loathing, and quite understandably.

Had Rasputin been a Russian teenager instead of a cat, he would have belonged to the Komsomol, or Young Communist League—his manners were that deplorable.

What is the most treacherous act that you can conceive of one cat committing against another? That's right. And that vile brute Rasputin did it to our tender little Henrietta, and right in the sanctity of her own home.

It happened one spring evening. I had just returned home for dinner and was alerted to the betrayal by Celia's screams.

"Rasputin's eating Henrietta's food!" she cried.

I rushed to the kitchen to catch Rasputin, who had jumped through the open window and muscled his way past Henrietta. Callously ignoring her wails and hisses, Rasputin had taken possession of her bowl of cat food, the contents of which had been imported from Helsinki at no small expense. And the hirsute scoundrel was greedily devouring it all.

I scooped up Rasputin and propelled him out the window with as much force as he had used to invade our kitchen. He smelled pretty ripe to me, so you can imagine Henrietta's revulsion. She demanded a clean bowl before we presented her with more food, which had to be from Finland.

This might be a good time to relate how our cat would walk down Petrovka Street past the imposing eight-columned Bolshoi Theater to Red Square and Lenin's Mausoleum, and enter the Kremlin under its dramatic Spassky Tower to slip unnoticed into a closed meeting of the ruling politburo, returning in time to brief me as to which old man among the Soviet Union's geriatric leadership was likeliest to be demoted to supervising some hydroelectric power station off in Central Asia.

But you would only scoff, knowing as well as I do that even a cat from New York City could not have undertaken such a journey to the Kremlin, given the hazards of getting run over or asphyxiated in Moscow's boisterous smoke-belching traffic.

This did not prevent me from shamelessly exploiting Henrietta to gather my news, though I didn't go so far as to carry her over to Red Square and describe her as a source close to the Kremlin.

One European diplomat I knew was destined for a career ambassadorship and couldn't admit to sharing confidences with the press. But he was willing to sit in our living room with Henrietta in his lap, stroking her while he discussed the significance of the latest power shift within the Kremlin and I took notes from an adjacent armchair.

From time to time, my knowledgeable diplomatic source would pause and ask, "Isn't that right, Henrietta?" (or, if you prefer, *"N'est-ce pas, Henriette?"*).

At the time, *The New York Times* had two correspondents, and sometimes just one, in Moscow to cover everything happening in the fifteen republics that then constituted the Soviet Union. And because Moscow time is eight hours ahead of New York (seven in summer), I got into the habit, common among foreign correspondents, of reporting a story during the day and not sitting down to write it until the evening.

This meant that I tended to leave the *Times* bureau after midnight. Jaqueline would be asleep; she had to rise early to send Celia and Chris off to the Anglo-American School, which was run by the English-speaking embassies in Moscow. So I would return home to be greeted by Henrietta, if she wasn't already curled up on one of the children's beds or off tracking mice.

One night as I was finishing up some reading in the living room, Henrietta's hunting growl alerted me to a curious commotion on the Ring Road outside our apartment. I followed the cat to the windowsill, where she crouched, ears alert, whiskers twitching, tail flapping to and fro. She seemed mesmerized by what she had seen.

An enormous bat was making its way down the nearly deserted eight-lane highway.

At least Henrietta appeared to think that it was a bat. A batwing MiG jet fighter was being towed from an undisclosed factory on one side of Moscow to some equally mysterious airfield on the other side. Leading the caravan was a police car whose loudspeaker squawked at the few cars still out at such a late hour to get out of the way.

"Henrietta," I told her, "try to catch a MiG, and we'll both get expelled."

In time, the postmidnight spectacle became commonplace enough that neither Henrietta nor I would have reacted unless the entire Soviet Air Force had been trundled past our apartment en route to the Western front.

When it came to other cats, though, Henrietta's curiosity was replete with jealousy. On one trip, I traveled through Siberia to the Russian Far East, where, after reporting some stories in Khabarovsk and Nakhodka, I caught a small steamer bound for the Japanese port of Yokahama. By the time I reached Japan, it was easier to continue eastward than to turn back through the Soviet Union, so I flew on to New York for a meeting with the foreign editor.

Before finally leaving for Moscow, I spent a night in New York with Jack, a friend with whom I'd started out in journalism some years earlier. His cat took an inordinate interest in my open bag. Whether the cat was attracted by the scent of Henrietta or mice in the succession of Siberian hotels where I had stayed, it added its contribution by spraying a scent of urine on the contents, which by then consisted mostly of dirty laundry.

I arrived home in Moscow, where Henrietta trotted out, tail high, to greet me. When she sniffed the open bag, she looked up at me with the distress of a woman who has just discovered lipstick smudging her husband's shirt collar. Henrietta foraged through my laundry for further signs of infidelity and added her own scent to ward off other cats: "Sorry, this one's taken." Thereafter whenever I returned from a reporting trip, Henrietta carefully checked out my luggage.

I was learning a fundamental difference between cats and dogs. When you introduce a couple of dogs, they will likely as not strike up an immediate friendship. After sniffing each other fore and aft, one dog will propose, "Wanna go chase some cars?" or "My owner planted a garden—you wanna help me dig it up?" and they'll romp off together as though they had been buddies since puppyhood.

But place two cats within sight or smell of each other, and the result is a staring or hissing contest—if the claws aren't out already.

At one point, Jaqueline decided that what Henrietta really

needed was a feline companion. Moscow's unofficial pet market had lots of kittens for sale, peeking out adorably from baskets or the folds of the vendor's overcoat. I didn't want another cat and thought that Henrietta would be threatened by its arrival.

I was proven right when the French Embassy's doctor was reassigned to a new posting and Jaqueline agreed to take in his elegant Siamese. When the interloper, all fur and flash, arrived in our apartment, Henrietta wanted nothing to do with it. She hissed and caterwauled so long and loud that the cowed Siamese was returned to sender the next day.

Henrietta preferred to select her own chums. I will concede that she had excellent taste. Her best friends in Moscow became the attractive young couple living in the apartment next door.

Valerio Astraldi, an Italian diplomat, was volubly amusing as well as politically savvy. His pretty Finnish wife, Marit, was a superb cook who has since published some best-selling cookbooks in Finland on Italian cuisine. Rather than sully her dishes with the inferior Russian pasta, Marit prepared linguine and spaghetti from scratch.

Needless to say, whenever the Astraldis invited us to dinner, we canceled any prior diplomatic engagements to accept, though I suspect that the invitation was made primarily for Henrietta's sake. While we dined on Marit's freshly made fettuccine with homemade pesto, Henrietta was spoiled with prosciutto or Parma ham that the Astraldis had brought back from Rome.

During the day, I sometimes encountered our cat stretched on a green wooden bench in the courtyard outside our apartment with our neighbor. Marit would be stroking Henrietta with one slender hand while the other balanced a book that she was reading in one of the half-dozen languages in which she was fluent.

Henrietta took to keeping vigil over the children's beds whenever they were suffering from one of the strains of colds or fevers that swept Moscow every winter. She was so reliable that Jaqueline nicknamed her the "gray nurse."

This did not amuse our grandmotherly Russian housekeeper, Tamara Mikhailovna, who was convinced that suffocation and death would result if Henrietta were permitted so close to the sleeping children. Tamara was hardly timid, having served in the Red Army as a teenage corporal against the Nazi invaders during World War II. When I looked into the origin of her folk wisdom, I found that such fears of cats were hardly confined to Russia.

You could go back four centuries to Edward Topsell and his authoritative (at the time) book *The History of Four Footed Beasts.* The English naturalist warned his readers "that the breath and savor of cats consume their radical humor and destroy the lungs, and they who keep the cats with them in their beds have the air corrupted and fall into hectics and consumptions."

Our children thrived on Henrietta's bedtime companionship, and we indulged our cat in ways that appalled some of our Russian friends. It is not startling news that an American pet manages to eat better than many people around the world, but this sobering truth never sunk in until we found ourselves living abroad.

When we first arrived in Moscow, I made the mistake of introducing Henrietta to some Russian caviar, the good stuff that gets exported for resale at obscene prices. Henrietta lapped up every last one of the tiny black fish eggs and demanded more. I envisioned her cultivating an extravagant palate that we couldn't afford, because even in Russia those little black eggs don't come cheap. Besides, feeding caviar to one's cat evoked the kind of gilded decadence associated with the aristocrats whose appalling excesses had made the Russian Revolution seem like not such a bad idea back in 1917.

So we weaned Henrietta onto a more affordable diet of canned salmon and sturgeon. Even these Russian-made staples were in short supply in ordinary Moscow stores. We had to import them from Helsinki, with their original "Made in the USSR" labels, or we had to procure them at the *beryozka,* a foreigners-only shop that demanded hard currency in the form of special coupons not available to ordinary Russians.

Tamara Mikhailovna was upset to see Henrietta being fed fancier food than most Muscovites could buy.

"Est odni lish' delikatessi," Tamara fumed. The cat eats only luxury foods.

To save face all around, we had to postpone feeding Henrietta her favorite salmon and sturgeon until evening, after Tamara had gone home.

It was not our only extravagance on Henrietta's behalf. Because the Russian milk sold in Moscow was unpasteurized at the time and rumored to come from tubercular cows, we imported our children's milk by rail from Finland. And invariably we ordered an extra liter for our cat.

We had to import stranger things from Stockmann's department store in Helsinki, down to Russian-made auto parts for the office Volga sedan. Auto parts were so scarce in the Soviet Union that when I parked on the street, I followed the example of every car-owning Muscovite: I removed the windshield wipers and locked them inside my car.

When we first arrived in Moscow, Celia and Chris turned on the black-and-white television set in our apartment. They were disappointed to find the programming dominated by harvest successes in Kazakhstan and coverage of Leonid Brezhnev, who was well on his way to becoming immortalized as the Soviet Communist Party's most tedious leader, notwithstanding stiff competition from other tired old men in the ruling politburo.

A popular riddle circulating while we lived in Moscow asked, "What has four legs, two long ears, and Brezhnev in the middle?" The answer: a television set.

So where is Leonid Brezhnev now that America's parents really need him? Defunct, alas. Because given the opportunity to watch Brezhnev on television at almost any hour, our children took to reading so voraciously that by the time Celia reached the seventh grade, she tested at the reading level of a high school senior. Chris, while several years younger, was devouring books at a similarly rapid rate.

Celia and Chris also spent their time after school staging plays with the other children at Sadovo-Samotechnaya. When Henrietta wandered in, she found herself launched on a fleeting thespian career as a costumed walk-on in their rainy-day repertory.

I returned home one day from my daily jog around Red Army Park to find Henrietta escaping the children's bedroom, which surprised me because she enjoyed napping there. Our cat trailed a gauzy white train, looking like a terrified bride fleeing her vows at the altar.

"What's happened to the cat?" I asked Celia, who was in pursuit of Henrietta.

"She's joined our cast of *The Littlest Angel,*" Celia said, "and left rehearsal without the director's permission."

The show, adapted very loosely from a children's book, premiered on schedule with sundry mothers and kids from Sadovo-Samotechnaya in attendance, but not Henrietta, who learned to make herself scarce whenever the costumes were pulled out.

Sadly, the performance unraveled after Chris got stage fright and balked at playing the title role in which Celia had cast him, objecting that the cardboard angel wings and bedsheet made him look like a sissy to his soccer-playing chums.

Instead, Chris set up a food concession, selling delicious milk shakes made with Russian ice cream, Jaqueline's chocolate sauce, and our limited supply of milk from Helsinki. At the ruble equivalent of twenty-two cents for a shake, Chris did such brisk business with the other children that we ran out of milk. I later calculated that I had lost a dollar on each milk shake. I never finished mine after learning that it had been tested on Henrietta.

To an outsider, our home life must sound cloyingly cute, but it illustrates how closely our family, Henrietta included, pulled together in the absence of the extraneous distractions, from television cartoons to shopping malls, that have come to dominate childhood in the United States.

We look back wistfully on those evenings in Moscow when the family's high spots became Jaqueline's homemade hot-fudge sundaes and the Sunday afternoons that we spent skiing together among the snow-shrouded birch trees along the Moscow River.

And we miss our periodic "breathers" to see the bright lights of Helsinki, sharing a snug four-passenger compartment on the midnight train that rolled across the dark expanse of northern Russia to the Finnish frontier, where we breakfasted on fresh doughnuts and hot coffee or cocoa while the train crews changed locomotives.

Having been raised in a family of itinerant actors, I had been taught to travel light and took packing as something of a challenge. I once wandered for several weeks through the Horn of Africa with a shoulder bag containing a typewriter, a camera, a spare shirt, some underwear and socks, and a blue drip-dry suit for interviewing whatever warlords I met, who by the end of my journey tended to stand well upwind of me.

Jaqueline, on the other hand, was born into a family that vacationed in France by sailing there and back first class. Her habit of packing generously for all occasions, formal or otherwise, was of little practical use after she married a journalist.

Though she worked hard to cut down, we invariably ended up with more suitcases than we could conveniently carry, plus, of course, Henrietta. I once spent a month on Mount Everest toting less gear than our family was accustomed to taking on a short holiday.

Jaqueline was loath to leave behind anything that the children might need, a category that ranged well beyond our cat. It's easy enough to leave something behind when you know that you can always buy it on arrival if you want it. But when the winter wind chapped Celia's lips on a trip to Leningrad (now called St. Petersburg), there was no lip balm to be found. So Jaqueline had to apply her own lipstick to ease Celia's discomfort. With good reason, Jaqueline balked at traveling light, even on vacation.

In addition to the usual clothing, Jaqueline packed lots of guidebooks about places we expected to visit, maps torn out of airline magazines, and workbooks from a correspondence school in Baltimore to supplement the children's continuing education. She carried along suntan lotion, dry penicillin and distilled water for earaches, a thermometer, fluoride pills, a sewing kit, aspirins, decongestants, playing cards, scissors, colored pencils, and the children's diaries, games, and toys.

An entire suitcase was devoted to what could be most graciously described as family clutter. This included letters that we kept meaning to answer, unopened bank statements and department-store bills, shopping catalogs, old copies of *The New York Times* and the *International Herald Tribune* that Jaqueline refused to throw out until she had read them—and what better time than during our vacation?

And for Henrietta, there was a bag with some dried and canned cat food, a couple of bowls, and a folding box with some cat litter.

One summer in Moscow, we decided to take our vacation in the Åland Islands, a wooded archipelago populated by Swedish-speaking Finns at the northern rim of the Baltic Sea.

To get there, we first had to cross the Soviet-Finnish border in our family's bright-red Zhiguli. This Soviet-made copy of a Fiat was marketed for a while in the West under the name Lada and became renowned for having (a) the ability to start on the coldest winter morning and (b) virtually no room to store anything.

The *Times* bureau's driver, Ivan Vasilivich, drove our red Zhiguli, stuffed with our luggage, up from Moscow and met our overnight train at Vyborg near the Finnish border. Before he caught the train back to Moscow, we repacked the car to carve out enough room inside for the Wren family, which meant tying a pyramid of suitcases and bags to a rack mounted on the roof.

When the Soviet border guards and customs officials saw us rolling down the nearly deserted road toward the frontier post, they sprang into action, suspecting that a Russian family was escaping to the West with everything it owned or had borrowed or stolen. We were frantically waved down, and at gunpoint.

The defenders of Russia's borders were not reassured to discover that I was an American newspaper correspondent.

"Are you departing the motherland permanently?" the chief of the frontier post inquired.

"Only for two weeks," Jaqueline assured him.

The chief inspector chuckled at her insolence, convinced that any family moving like beasts of burden could not be taking a two-week vacation.

Displaying the sophistication that might be expected from someone who grew up thinking of shoes mass-produced in Bulgaria as haute couture, the chief inspector went to work on a craftier theory: we had deliberately overladen ourselves to conceal some contraband, perhaps an antique brass samovar or an ikon dating back to Peter the Great and therefore prohibited for export.

Or worse, we must have taken it upon ourselves to smuggle out manuscripts for our dissident writer friends. That sort of suspicion later prompted the Soviet authorities to accuse me of spying, without bothering to contrive convincing evidence.

So our possessions were pulled from the car and strewn along the Karelian roadside. The inspectors made us open every suitcase and bag, one by one. They pulled out bathing suits, flip-flops, rain parkas, and sweaters.

They thumbed through our children's books in English, scrutinizing the potentially subversive dialectics of Paddington Bear, Pippi Longstocking, and Winnie-the-Pooh.

The inspectors sniffed, squeezed, and tasted their way through the contents of Jaqueline's kit of traveling medicine. They peeled the lining out of my alarm clock.

The border guards were not standing idle. Slinging their assault rifles, they poked mirrors mounted on broom handles under the little Zhiguli and pulled up the carpeting inside.

"You have no ikons to declare?" the chief inspector asked with increasing incredulity. "No manuscripts? Samovars? Weapons?"

Jaqueline assured him that we carried the usual things that an American family would find indispensable for a holiday at the beach.

After three hours of fruitless searching, the inspectors wearily threw up their hands. They left us to repack our car—without their assistance—and let us proceed across the Finnish frontier, but not before their chief gave us a finger-wagging lecture.

"You must learn to travel with less stuff!" he snapped.

Jaqueline would, I'm sure, beg to point out that it rained constantly during our stay in the Åland Islands, so everything she insisted upon taking, except for the bathing suits and suntan lotion, did get used.

Such brusque encounters with the Soviet bureaucracy did not extend to Henrietta's relations with ordinary Russians, among whom I would include the officials who had rallied to facilitate her clearance through Sheremetyevo airport when she first arrived. Most Russians display such a soft spot for cats that it may be a national characteristic.

Russian cat fanciers of note included Aleksandr Borodin, chemistry professor and composer of the opera *Prince Igor,* which is best known for its "Polovetsian Dances." (To summon it up, whistle a few bars of the pop hit "Stranger in Paradise.")

According to his fellow composer Nikolai Rimsky-Korsakov, Borodin's cats were not shy about clambering on to the dinner table and sticking their noses in the plates of the guests. One of his cats had a habit of fetching home stray kittens, for which Borodin abandoned his piano to find them good homes. Whether or not he threw in a bottle of vodka is one of those details better left to the historians.

So it's not surprising that Henrietta would extend her paw to welcome the dissident physicist Andrei Dmitriyevich Sakharov when he and his wife, Yelena Bonner, came around for dinner one night.

Sakharov was a brilliant nuclear physicist who developed the Soviet Union's hydrogen bomb before taking his courageous stand as the country's leading human rights advocate, for which he was awarded the Nobel Peace Prize.

"Don't let the kids or the cat pester him," I told Jaqueline before driving over to fetch the Sakharovs. "He's got more important things to think about."

Though I had visited their apartment dozens of times before inviting the Sakharovs to dinner, I failed to realize that nothing was too unimportant to escape the kind nature of Andrei Dmitriyevich. No sooner did they arrive than Sakharov, a scientist of engaging shyness, headed straight for our children's cluttered bedroom. There he proceeded to assemble their Tinkertoys to demonstrate for Celia and Chris what an atom looked like, while I looked on open-mouthed at the fun they all were having.

It took some time to pry Sakharov away from the Tinkertoys and sit him down in our living room, where Henrietta was waiting in ambush. The cat showed herself capable of behaving like a shameless coquette around Nobel Prize laureates.

Before I could shoo her off, Henrietta hopped up into his lap and presented first her ears, then her belly for scratching. Sakharov was delighted to oblige, chatting away in his uniquely lisping Russian, not to me but to Henrietta, *milaya koshka.* Dear little cat.

Henrietta also charmed our other Russian friends when we took her visiting. Sometimes we drove outside Moscow to a friend's *dacha,* or weekend cottage, in a suburban area closed to foreigners. I packed snow over the office Volga sedan's coded license plate, which identified me as a K-4, meaning an American correspondent. The Soviet security establishment wanted Western reporters to be readily identifiable to Russians as *inostrantsy,* or potentially dangerous foreigners. My cover was blown when the host invited all his neighbors over to meet an authentic American cat, which they found vastly more interesting than an authentic American correspondent.

When it came time to take Henrietta to the local Russian veterinarian, things turned a little more traumatic. The veterinarian began his checkup by swaddling Henrietta snugly in a large pink bandage until she looked rather like a sausage, with little more than her head, furry rear, and tail protruding. Russians traditionally swaddled their babies in like fashion, so they did not view treating a cat this way as cruel or unusual.

Henrietta protested the humiliation of this ignominious posture, but it did her no good. The Russian veterinarian hoisted our cat on a scale, weighed her like a grocer weighing a sack of potatoes, and, with her restrained from squirming unduly, jabbed a syringe filled with antirabies vaccine into her rear before unwinding the bandage and releasing her into our custody.

By now Henrietta was no mere pet but an active member of our family. Yet it embarrassed me to admit that she remained more skittish of me than of many Russians she had met, realizing perhaps that I had opposed bringing her to Moscow. This subtle estrangement ended abruptly one Sunday in September, after I was assaulted while covering an art show.

I had gone off to Moscow's southwestern outskirts to see an unofficial exhibition of dissident art set up in an empty lot near the Belyayevo subway station. I was talking with some artists when a bunch of husky strangers, who turned out to be Soviet cops in civilian clothes, arrived and set about breaking up the exhibition, quite literally. One man driving a bulldozer knocked over the paintings. His colleagues fed some canvases into a bonfire they had built. The artists who protested or stood their ground were roughed up or taken away to the local precinct.

I tried to take a photograph of the unprovoked attack and had my Nikon camera slammed into my teeth. Then, while two plainclothes thugs pinned my arms behind my back, a third thug slammed his beefy fist into my stomach just below the belt.

I returned home with a story to write, but the truth is that I didn't feel much like writing it. One of my front teeth was chipped, and the rest of my mouth ached. My stomach hurt too. There was no point calling the police; my assailants had been the police. When I telephoned the doctor at the American Embassy, he said that unless I had blood in my urine, the assault sounded like something that would not require his professional services.

Jaqueline was worried, of course. "You ought to lie down," she said. "We'll go to Helsinki to have Dr. Gran"—our Finnish dentist—"fix your teeth."

I protested that I had to write my eyewitness account of the senseless demolition of the art exhibit. But I followed my solicitous wife's orders, and she agreed to wake me in an hour.

Of course, I couldn't sleep. I lay across our double bed feeling as sorry for myself as for the artists who had had their safety as well as their art violated. I wondered whether to send a message to the foreign desk that I was too banged up from the assault to file myself, and ask them to run an account from the wire agencies.

And then I felt something hop softly on the bed. I opened my eyes and saw Henrietta creeping up silently alongside me. She liked to curl up with the children and Jaqueline but had never seen fit to favor me with such a visit.

I shut my eyes again and felt Henrietta rub against my leg and nestle down against my hip. Then I heard her purr.

I reached down and lightly caressed the soft fur along her neck. She snuggled in tighter until my sore mouth and gut no longer throbbed. There is something consoling about stroking a pet when you feel frightened and alone. For the first time, it was clear that Henrietta and I belonged together.

Her purring continued for some time, reminding me over and over, "Don't let human nature get you down."

After a while, Henrietta got up and sprang off the bed. She's right, I thought, we've both got better things to do. I walked across the courtyard to the office, sat down, and wrote my account of the destruction of the art exhibit. The *Times* featured it across the front page the next morning and later flew me to Helsinki to get my teeth fixed.

What more can I say, except that thereafter Henrietta and I got along famously?

Some readers, upon learning that our cat spent four years living under Soviet communism, which began to unravel only after her departure, will be pressing for the answer to a puzzle that continues to intrigue serious students of Kremlinology:

"What role," you may well ask, "did Henrietta play in the collapse of the Soviet Union?"

Actually, nobody ever put the question that bluntly, but it is not as farfetched as some of the theories floating out there. If Ronald Reagan can get credit for dumping the Soviet Union onto the dustbin of history, why not Henrietta, who was on the ground, after all, and in a position to do some tangible damage?

Let's review the evidence. Henrietta consorted daily with an American correspondent in Moscow. She refused to denounce her master after he was accused of being a lackey of Western intelligence agencies and filmed while jogging through Red Army Park in a bright-blue track suit on the pretext of getting fit, though everyone knows he must have been racing to meet religious dissidents somewhere off camera!

Henrietta accepted bribes of sturgeon and cabbage from Russians who expressed their hatred of the Commmunist system. She submitted to the caresses of Andrei D. Sakharov, whose activism on behalf of human rights won him the Nobel Peace Prize. She purred sympathetically for numerous other dissidents who were caught on camera visiting our apartment.

Henrietta committed an act of sabotage against a giant crane that was needed to construct communism, because she was observed peeing against its base and thereby causing it to rust away.

Under the pretense of poking into embassy garbage cans, the American cat trotted brazenly about Moscow as a hireling of the Central Intelligence Agency, assassinating mice loyal to the Communist Party, and committing many other sinister acts of an anti-Soviet nature on instructions from the fat cats of Wall Street.

Ridiculous, you say? In Moscow, we came to know stubborn dissenters such as Aleksandr Ginsburg and Anatoly (Natan) Sharansky, who were arrested and dispatched to hard labor in Siberia on flimsier charges. Our closest friends, Veniamin and Tanya Levich, lost their scientific honors, their careers, and nearly their son Yevgeny, who was sent to a penal battalion in the Arctic because his parents dared apply to emigrate to Israel. The Soviet Union collapsed after gutsy people like these refused to participate in the lie that Marxism-Leninism was the inevitable future for us all.

But in apportioning the lion's share of the blame, let's not forget the gang in the Kremlin that couldn't rule straight; they hijacked the opportunity for democracy given by the czar's abdication in 1917 and rewarded loyal patriots by dispatching millions of them to prison camps. The Soviet Communist Party leaders bankrupted their country by squandering its wealth on all the wrong things, including themselves.

It does not take a Henrietta to understand the proverb that "a fish rots from the head down." In the end, a whisk of her tail could have sufficed to topple the corrupt edifice of Soviet-style communism.

So in analyzing Henrietta's contribution to this welcome development, let me sound statesmanlike, by which I mean as equivocal as the U.S. State Department, and reply: "As for my cat's reported role in hastening the Soviet Union's demise, I have looked thoroughly into these rumors and am in a position to neither confirm nor deny them."

Rome

During our four years in Moscow—that window on Marxism-Leninism as it lurched toward Utopia—fresh produce was in such short supply in state shops that an orange or banana qualified as a luxury. Down at the store for foreigners only, the *beryozka,* we forked over dollars to buy scarce items unavailable for rubles to ordinary Russians. But even there, the canned Bulgarian peas resembled olive-drab buckshot. The orange juice was canned in Algeria and poured like the goo that drips from your car when the oil is changed. During our final winter, even Algeria's export-quality orange sludge vanished from Moscow's shelves.

The material shortages in our lives were compounded by the constant surveillance of the KGB and bizarre accusations of spying. "Your questions are not those of a Soviet journalist," one flinty-eyed KGB flack explained. I was touched, because you don't get compliments like that every day.

Our family, and here I include Henrietta, grew eager to wallow again in the decadent delights of the capitalist West. So when I learned that Craig Whitney, the *Times* bureau chief in Bonn, would be replacing me in Moscow, I proposed a simple swap to my editors.

I had visited Berlin during a reporting swing through Eastern Europe the previous autumn and had been reminded how well things work in West Germany. The beer was delicious. The tidy shops overflowed with a veritable cornucopia of goodies awaiting the arrival of *die Katze,* as the Germans would call our Henrietta.

And the Bonn bureau had just bought a Mercedes sedan in robin's-egg blue. The Moscow bureau's dirty white Volga sedan, another Russian model larger than our family's red Zhiguli, drove like a tank, though it did start in winter, which was what mattered.

My evaluation of the Moscow bureau's Volga has been challenged by Malcolm Browne, who as the *Times* correspondent in Belgrade covered my absences from Moscow and spoiled Henrietta whenever he filled in. Mal had driven a tank in the U.S. Army and found the Volga's handling much inferior.

My editors agreed that sending me to Bonn when Craig came to Moscow was a novel idea. But they proposed that I consider an alternative scenario.

"Oranges," one editor promised.

"What about them?" I asked.

"Sunshine and oranges. Egypt has lots of oranges, and other fresh fruit and vegetables that you haven't seen in Moscow. Why not take over our Cairo bureau, because we're sending Henry Tanner to Rome?"

I admit that I salivated at the prospect of a juicy orange.

"Uh-uh," I messaged back to New York, but politely. I had visited Cairo on a reporting assignment seven years earlier and remembered the sand and trash. But, I hinted, there was always Bonn.

I didn't hear back from my editors, which appeared to settle the matter. I ordered a German phrase book from Helsinki and began testing it out on *die Katze.*

The next communication on the matter came via Interdean, an internationally known German moving company. So many German stamps were pasted on the envelope that I had no doubt where we were bound. I opened the packet.

"The New York Times has selected us to move your household goods to Cairo," the letter inside began. Enclosed were enough forms to wallpaper the bathroom of our Moscow apartment. They had to be filled out in triplicate and returned before the moving van arrived in a few weeks.

I telexed the *Times* foreign desk to sound the alarm.

"Some pushy German moving company is threatening to pack off everything I own to Cairo, including my wife, our kids and the family cat," I wrote. "Does anyone at your end know whether this is relevant to my next assignment?"

The prompt reply was so delicious that I regret not having saved a copy, so I shall try to re-create the contents.

"No final decision has been made," I was assured, "but we hope that you will consider going to Cairo, which has lots of sunshine and fresh fruit and vegetables."

In response, I lied that I would give the Cairo bureau some thought.

The editors called my bluff, proposing that I fly down to Cairo and look over my new beat before making up my mind.

"Lots of time," they cheerfully concluded.

By my calculations, Interdean's moving van would shortly be crossing the Polish-Soviet border and rolling eastward through Brest-Litovsk and Minsk toward Moscow, gathering greater momentum than Napoleon's legions and Hitler's panzer divisions had achieved in their disastrous invasions.

I responded like any level-headed *Times* correspondent: I drove the paunchy Volga down to the Aeroflot office and booked a flight to Cairo, round-trip. Jaqueline, meanwhile, had begun filling in the voluminous forms for the German movers.

The news had to be broken to Henrietta. "How would you

like to go to Cairo instead?" I asked her when she popped in through our kitchen window after her daily inspection of the Central Market. "It has all kinds of sunshine," I told her, "and oranges and vegetables."

Henrietta was unimpressed, preferring to concentrate on the can of Russian sturgeon that I had scooped into her food bowl.

"And new mice," I added. Henrietta had accomplished such a thorough extermination in our apartment that that the only mice we had seen of late were dancing in the corps de ballet of *The Nutcracker* down at the Bolshoi Theater.

Already the sophisticated traveler, our cat raised no objection to this sudden change of itinerary.

So I flew to Cairo, which looked much better than I had remembered it, though I did not share this pleasant discovery with my editors at the *Times.* The city bustled with colorful if noisy activity. Cairo was filled with smiles and laughter that contrasted with the sullen drabness of Moscow.

As promised, Cairo's market stalls overflowed with fresh oranges, lemons, mangoes, tomatoes, and dates, all of them picked at the peak of ripeness and sold for a pittance compared with what we had to pay in Moscow or even New York.

For Henrietta, there were fish freshly caught from the Nile or the Mediterranean, flapping on the vendors' scales.

That settled the matter. Before returning to Moscow, I rented a three-bedroom apartment in Zamalek, a residential neighborhood of old colonial mansions and newer precarious high-rises on Gezira, an island smack in the middle of the Nile. The apartment I found was in a state of shambles, but the jolly landlord swore that it would be renovated into first-class shape once I forked over a very large security deposit. Housing was scarce in Cairo, and the apartment in Zamalek did have sunlit balconies from every bedroom, giving Henrietta a choice of views.

By now no one at the *Times* had ordered me to go to Cairo. But how could I not consider going when it offered all kinds of sunshine, fresh fruit, vegetables, and so on—and the assurance of a continuing paycheck that would not require me to cover shopping malls on Staten Island?

While I was grinding out my final articles from Moscow, much of the logistical nightmare of moving fell on Jaqueline's shoulders. There was a triage involved: a limited amount of possessions could travel with us; other things could follow by airfreight; and the rest, including books, what little furniture we had, and dishware, would arrive by sea a few months later—or many months later if it were shipped via the Canary Islands, Paraguay, Borneo, Mauritius, and the Seychelles.

This required Jaqueline to make a succession of spot decisions for the movers who rolled through our apartment packing and labeling the cartons. Over the course of nineteen years, Jaqueline struggled with such moves eight times before we returned to New York for good, and while she became increasingly more proficient at it, the ordeal never got easier.

Henrietta, on the other hand, loved moving from country to country. As soon as the suitcases were opened, she would climb into one and refuse to budge. And while our cat emitted the usual pro forma squawks upon being deposited in her traveling case, it did not take long before she calmed down and settled back to enjoy the passing view through the window screen.

Celia and Chris were assigned the essential task of preparing Henrietta for her move. Their job was more serious than keeping her from getting underfoot of the burly movers or consoling her that the chaos at hand would pass.

Like many other cats, Henrietta loved concealing herself in small, inaccessible nooks. She had a particular knack for squeezing inside the packing boxes that became as commonplace as furniture during our years abroad.

I was always afraid that Henrietta would crawl deep into a cardboard box and awake from her nap to find herself sealed in by the movers and loaded onto a van headed in an entirely different direction from the rest of her family.

We would have been bound to notice her absence later, of course, but unloading and unpacking all the boxes to find which one the cat had chosen would have set back our departure considerably. No one, least of all Jaqueline, wanted to go through the hell of doing the same packing twice.

In the course of our moves, Celia was given another task, as the vaccine courier. Henrietta's rabies shots seemed a formality in the United States. But in Russia and our subsequent postings, they were essential for moving her from one country to another. In Moscow, we usually imported the cat's vaccine from New York or Helsinki, the local vaccines being, like so many other Soviet products, scarce as well as unreliable. When it came time to update her inoculations, Henrietta endured more swaddling by her Russian veterinarian, unless he was busy and we could prevail upon the American Embassy doctor to inject her.

In Moscow and thereafter, whenever our family returned from a trip to the United States, Celia carried back the rabies vaccine in a bag packed with ice to keep it from spoiling.

In midflight, Celia would go to the lavatory and pour the melted ice water out of the vaccine bag. Once back in her seat, she would sweetly ask the stewardess for a soft drink with plenty of ice, which she would surreptitiously add to the vaccine bag. It was easier than explaining why she was toting the vaccine in the first place. Once we were back in Moscow, and later Cairo and Beijing, Henrietta's vaccine was stored in a corner of our refrigerator.

While we stuffed the final items into our bulging bags in preparation for leaving Russia, dear Tamara Mikhailovna sat in a chair, sobbing uncontrollably at the thought of never seeing Celia and Chris again. They would miss her too, but for now they were preoccupied with not losing sight of Henrietta. Scores of boxes had already been taped up and carted off to the Interdean van. This would not have been a good time for Henrietta to pay a farewell visit to her peasant friends down at the Central Market.

To recover from the exhaustion of the move, we decided to stop over in Rome for a week and a half of eating, sleeping, and sightseeing before continuing on to Cairo, where I would have to go immediately to work learning the political complexities of the Middle East.

By now Henrietta strenuously objected to being checked in to the hold with the rest of our luggage. So we asked Alitalia in advance to let our cat accompany us on the flight to Rome. For a nominal fee of fifty dollars or so, almost all the American carriers and some international ones will permit a single cat to ride inside the cabin if the place is booked sufficiently ahead.

What airlines try to avoid are two cats on board who may take an instant dislike to each other and start brawling and screeching in the aisles or under the seats, particularly during takeoffs and landings, while the crew is overwhelmed with the challenge of getting seat belts tightened, tray tables stowed, and everyone returned to his or her upright position.

One can hardly quarrel with this policy, the cautionary logic of which becomes apparent in a familiar limerick:

> There once were two cats from Kilkenny,
> Which each thought was one cat too many,
> So they fought and they fit,
> And they scratched and they bit,
> 'Til except for their nails
> And the tips of their tails,
> Instead of two cats there weren't any.

Because if one dueling feline were to chase the other into the airplane cockpit, there might not be any passengers left over either.

The good news is that a traveling cat who makes an intelligent choice of airline well in advance can anticipate the kind of service that is seldom extended to most passengers these days, except in magazine advertisements.

The Alitalia crew cordially welcomed Henrietta aboard our flight from Moscow and later flattered her palate by delivering a complementary portion of the delicious in-flight appetizer: salmon mousse topped with a perky boiled shrimp and served on a lettuce leaf.

Henrietta showed off her good manners by leaving the lettuce leaf uneaten.

Our flight took off from Moscow behind schedule, dallied in Milan, and didn't land in Rome until nearly midnight. Arriving late at Fiumicino International Airport, we needed some time to explain to Italian immigration and customs why our baggage carts were piled with twenty-one suitcases and cargo bags plus *il gatto,* as Italians call Henrietta, when our airline tickets made it clear that we planned to stay in Italy for only a week.

Henrietta had acquired a sturdy wooden traveling case purchased from the Royal Society for Prevention of Cruelty to Animals when she first passed through Heathrow International Airport in London. Just as she had done at Moscow's Sheremetyevo airport nearly four years earlier, she expedited our clearance through Italian customs with some plaintive and well-timed meowing.

We needed two taxis to carry us the more than twenty miles into Rome from Fiumicino. But only one was in sight. That would mean ferrying our baggage in two trips and not getting to bed much before dawn. But the taxi driver, who was surprisingly helpful considering the late hour, promised to accomplish it in a single journey. He set Henrietta carefully on the front seat and then started jamming our luggage into the Fiat's small trunk, on top of Henrietta's box, and finally on top of us too.

Henrietta protested this intrusion into her traveling space, and the driver bent low to soothe her concerns in Italian.

"Sì, il gatto," he cooed. *"Bel gatto, bello, bello . . ."* Beautiful cat.

His melodic singing and *tsk-tsk*s would have been more endearing had our taxi not been hurtling toward Rome at something well beyond the hundred-kilometer mark. The speedometer was just about all I could see with two bags and one child piled on top of me.

"Not so fast, *per favore,*" I pleaded.

"Fast, fast? *Sì, sì, rapido.*" The speedometer edged up.

Henrietta only meowed more loudly.

"*Gatto, gatto mio. Tsk, tsk,"* the driver said. *"Il bellissimo gatto."*

Without taking his foot off the accelerator, the driver pressed his face down against Henrietta's cage. Some ostentatious kissing sounds followed. I think that Jaqueline asked him to slow down too, but I may have imagined it, since nothing of the sort happened.

"Gatto, gatto." Kiss, kiss, kiss. *"Bellissimo gatto."*

As this operatic duet between Henrietta and the taxi driver reached concert-level pitch, the taxi seemed to swerve to left and right, suggesting that we must at last be weaving through Rome's narrow seats.

The driver cooed into Henrietta's cage, *"Gatto, bel gatto."*

At last the driver, or what little I could see of him, sat bolt upright and slammed on the brakes. I braced for a crash, but no, we had merely arrived at our hotel overlooking the Villa Borghese.

The hotel did not object to having Henrietta as a guest. But the maid was terrified of her and refused to make the beds while Henrietta was around. On our third or fourth day, we returned to find the beds made and the cat nowhere to be seen.

Had the maid wreaked revenge by dropping Henrietta down the laundry chute?

We searched for several hours, not only in the room but in the corridor, on the stairway, and even on the tiled roof outside our window. Eventually, we did find Henrietta. She had squeezed into a hole in the mattress ticking and curled up inside it.

Jaqueline had a change of venue in mind. "Henrietta," she said, "how would you like to go see Saint Francis of Assisi?"

For all the saint's expansive love of animals, I'm afraid our cat had never heard of him or his hometown. However, the prospect appeared to interest Henrietta. She was bored playing hide-and-seek with the housekeeping staff at the Park Borghese, and Assisi was near enough to Rome that it seemed a shame not to let her pay her respects to her patron saint.

I rented a tiny Fiat, and we all drove with Henrietta to Assisi, which we were pleased to find nearly deserted of tourists in the off-season. Henrietta enjoyed the Subasio Hotel, whose floor tiles provided terrific opportunities for pouncing and sliding.

We ate our breakfast on a vine-covered terrace looking out on the Basilica of Saint Francis. Henrietta, never much for bread and cheese, preferred bits of prosciutto that we bought from a nearby store on the Via Frate Elia. She had gotten her palate for prosciutto from the Astraldis, our neighbors in Moscow.

Saint Francis, whom Henrietta could relate to eight centuries later, preached such love of nature and animals that he would never have objected to letting her visit his remains down in the basilica's crypt. But the Italian authorities were less broad-minded. Contrary to my hopes, we had to tour the church without our cat, while she stayed in the car. But we were rewarded by the marvelous Giotto frescoes in the basilica and the nearby church of Santa Chiara, one of which showed Saint Francis feeding some birds, though I can't recall that Giotto painted any cats into his frescoes.

What followed that day came very close to winding up our travels with Henrietta.

On the way back to Rome, we decided to have lunch in Orvieto, a medieval hill town that produces my favorite Italian white wine. Since we would have to leave Henrietta in the car, we stopped beforehand to let the cat perform her toilette in the tufted grass by the roadside. By now she was restless again, and she slipped the leash that Jaqueline had put on her by wriggling out of the collar as adroitly as Houdini.

Ignoring Celia's and Chris's frantic pleas to return, Henrietta galloped off to explore the fields of Umbria and soon vanished from sight altogether. For all she knew, Umbria was where we were going to put down roots again, and she had to check it out.

We had a problem more serious than missing our pasta and wine at a trattoria in Orvieto: we were scheduled to fly the next morning to Cairo, where we would be met by the *Times* bureau's assistant, Gamal Mohieddin. Gamal knew enough airport officials to prevent us from getting bogged down in customs with an itinerant cat and too much luggage. Canceling our flight and asking Alitalia to make new arrangements to carry a quantity of excess baggage normally associated with a television news crew, and to reserve cabin privileges for Henrietta, was something that I didn't want to fret about, though I did.

We couldn't be sure that we would find Henrietta, who had left Jaqueline holding the cat's collar with her identity tag. And since I had already lingered between postings, how could I tell the *Times* that I didn't know when I would get around to working in Cairo because I was remaining in Italy indefinitely to recover a lost cat?

The only other option left was for me to proceed to Cairo alone, leaving Jaqueline and the children behind to roam from village to village, asking about our cat. But then who would deal with all our luggage? Moreover, Celia and Chris were enrolled to start at their new school in Egypt the following Monday.

These thoughts ran through my mind with chilling clarity

as I ran across fields newly shorn of their crops, calling to a cat that I could no longer see.

It was sheer luck that I caught sight of Henrietta. She was resting under an impenetrably thick hedge. I lay down and groped under it, but even on my back, I was unable to reach her.

"You'll be singing for your supper in Italian if we leave you," I reminded her.

Jaqueline and the children, who by now were in tears, joined me. I don't know whether Henrietta realized that she would be left behind or was simply reassured to see the rest of her family, but she made no further moves to evade us.

Gently, Jaqueline coaxed Henrietta out from under the hedge, scooped her up, and carried her back to the Fiat. The children trotted merrily alongside, trying to pet her. I needed a glass of wine.

"I'm not going through that again," I told Jaqueline over our leisurely bottle of Orvieto's vino classico. I was wrong, of course.

Cairo

From history's perspective, describing Egypt as cat-friendly is like saying that Switzerland welcomes bank deposits. It was here, according to archaeologists, that cats first wandered in from the desert and deigned to become domesticated, a good four or five thousand years ago.

So Henrietta deserved to feel at home in Egypt, where back in the old days cats got some real respect. The ancient Egyptians were so solicitous of their cats that anyone who killed one, even by accident, risked being punished with death, or at least a very heavy fine. For many years, the export of cats to other countries was forbidden, in part, I suppose, because they had become Egypt's secret weapon for keeping rats away from the kingdom's stored grain.

The Greek historian Herodotus, when he visited Egypt twenty-five hundred years ago, remarked upon this Egyptian fondness for cats. "If a cat dies a natural death," he reported, "all the inmates of the house shave their eyebrows" as a sign of mourning.

Some centuries later, a Roman visitor named Diodorus reported that if someone killed a cat in Egypt, "he is certainly put to death, for the common people gather in crowds and deal with the perpetrator most cruelly, sometimes doing this without waiting for a trial."

Because of this public penchant for lynching cat killers, Diodorus continued, "any who have caught sight of one of these animals lying dead withdraw to a great distance and shout with lamentations and protestations that they found the animal already dead."

The fervor of the Egyptian populace had declined by the time we settled into Cairo, where within a few weeks curiosity nearly killed our cat.

I was preoccupied with getting my unfamiliar new beat into motion while not abandoning Jaqueline, who was appalled at the state of our rented apartment in Zamalek. The landlord had done nothing to clean it up since I had handed him the security deposit, evidently spending it on other frivolities.

When I reminded him of our deal, he replied, "I didn't know when you were coming," and pasted on his most charming smile.

Within days, water from defective plumbing was trickling into the apartment and stood ankle-deep in the bathroom. The landlord was considerate enough to have his servants lay down a couple planks for us to walk on to take our baths.

Then, one evening, Henrietta failed to show up for her supper.

At first we searched our apartment and the building, calling her name. Then I walked around the street and finally the entire neighborhood.

But Henrietta did not reappear.

Jaqueline and I tried to hide our worry from the children, explaining that the cat was doubtless off exploring, as she had done in Italy a few weeks earlier. Though Henrietta loved to explore, she invariably came back to be fed and probably would have done so if we had simply camped out in the fields of Umbria.

Now, however hard we looked, we couldn't find a trace of her.

With the help of the resourceful Cairo bureau assistant,

PRESS

Gamal Mohieddin, we offered rewards to all the doormen and street vendors in our neighborhood in Zamalek, galvanizing them to join our search for the *quttah,* as our cat was called in Egyptian Arabic.

Cairenes tend to swallow their guttural *q*'s, so they would nod and reply, *uttah.*

After a week or so, our search parties conjectured that Henrietta had been snatched up and cooked into shish kebab or else run over in the chaotic traffic careening along Zamalek's Twenty-sixth of July Street. Even Gamal, whose cheerful resourcefulness has saved the sanity of many a *Times* reporter, conceded that the cat's return looked improbable at best.

The search wound down for lack of leads, though we could not bring ourselves to call it off. We had no illusions about the dwindling prospects for her return.

We could no longer put off telling Celia and Chris that the cat was gone for good. When Jaqueline picked them up from school one afternoon, she broke the news as gently as she could.

Henrietta had disappeared for good, Jaqueline said. She paused and added that by now their cat might be dead.

But in their bedtime prayers every night, Celia and Chris kept asking that Henrietta not only be kept safe but be guided back to her family. Their faith seemed touching, but I thought it cruel to raise the children's expectations. While anything was possible, I told them, our cat's recovery looked more and more unlikely, given the hazards she faced on the unfamiliar streets. After all, Henrietta had only just arrived in Egypt and would be disoriented by the strange sounds and smells around our new home.

Yes, the cat was wearing her collar, but its heart-shaped tag bore our old address in Moscow, and that would be no help a continent away. We had been so busy getting settled in Cairo that we had not had time to order a new tag in Arabic.

I did not tell Celia and Chris that some cats, when they get separated from their owners, instinctively return to the home they remember best, because it would not be the new apartment in Zamalek. My mind conjured up visions of faithful little Henrietta walking across the desert to Alexandria with the burning sand singeing her paws, stowing aboard a freighter bound for the Black Sea, jumping off in the port of Odessa, and then padding northward for weeks across the Ukraine and Russia until she reached Moscow and the familiar courtyard at Sadovo-Samotechnaya, only to find that her incredible journey yielded no sign of our children.

That scenario, of course, was implausible. The best we could hope for, I concluded, was that someone else in Cairo would take Henrietta in and treat her kindly, which was by no means assured. Whoever found our cat could not send her back, I said, because even she did not know where she lived.

The following month, I flew to Tunis to cover a meeting of the Arab League, more preoccupied with Henrietta's loss than with the rambling speech that President Anwar el-Sadat had delivered a couple of nights earlier to the Egyptian Parliament. Sadat had a knack for hyperbolic rhetoric, so who believed his pledge to travel to Israel if that was what it took to bring peace to the Middle East?

I reported Sadat's speech but downplayed his bizarre notion of traveling to Jerusalem and confronting the Israelis in their own Knesset. I suppose that all journalists have made calls that we'd prefer to forget.

Even so, the Arab potentates who descended on the Tunis Hilton expressed outrage that Sadat would even consider breaking solidarity with his Arab brothers. The Arab League passed a few ineffectual resolutions castigating the Zionist enemy, and the conference dribbled to a conclusion.

Before flying back to Cairo, I went off with my friend Don Schanche of the *Los Angeles Times* to visit Tunis's marvelous *souk,* or bazaar, which offers some of the world's most colorful assortments of stuff you really don't need and a few things you do. I wanted to find some special present for Celia and Chris to help assuage the loss of their cat.

Among the woolen cloaks, carpets, tablecloths, coffee urns, camel blankets, and other tourist kitsch, I came upon a row of elegant Tunisian birdcages fashioned from filigreed wire. They seemed to be exactly what I was looking for. I would bring the children back a cage for a songbird, which I would help them buy after my return to Cairo.

I didn't want a grungy Egyptian cat replacing Henrietta on the rebound. But a bird suddenly seemed the most portable of pets for a foreign correspondent and his family. It would be low maintenance, and when my posting in the Middle East wound up, we could open the cage door in the direction of Rome or Bangkok or Buenos Aires or wherever the *Times* dispatched us next and simply let the bird fly there on its own. If it met us on arrival without the usual customs fuss, so much the better.

At first I considered two cages but dismissed this as logistically too difficult. Instead, I selected a single, more spacious birdcage, painted dazzling white with a light-blue trim. It would just about fit on my lap during the two-hour flight back to Cairo.

I returned to the hotel swinging my birdcage to find an urgent advisory from the foreign desk. The wire agencies were reporting that Sadat, who had skipped the Arab League summit, was now threatening to fly to Damascus to consult Syria's strongman, Hafez el-Assad, about going to Jerusalem. The *Times* wanted me in Damascus in time to cover the hugs and kisses that Arab leaders exchange when they cordially loathe each other.

This confronted me with the choice of carrying the children's birdcage to Damascus—and looking really silly—or leaving it behind in Tunis. Political wisdom suggested that Assad, a hard-line thug, would try to talk Sadat out of his quixotic trip to Jerusalem. I would be back in Cairo in a couple of days.

So the birdcage traveled with me to Damascus.

It did evoke snickers from the gaggle of Middle East reporters who had chased Sadat to Damascus. We spent most of our time doing what grown-ups in journalism tend to do, which was standing around for hours outside closed doors waiting for some fatuous flunky to pop out and say something unintelligible so we could race one another to the hotel telex machine and fight over the privilege of filing the story first.

On this occasion, Assad publicly hugged and kissed Sadat, from which we inferred that the Syrian dictator was thoroughly annoyed at Sadat for even thinking about going to Jerusalem. And Sadat resolved to go anyway to spite his brother-in-arms, though we didn't learn this until midnight.

While Jerusalem lies 140 miles south of Damascus as the cruise missile flies, the road was blocked with land mines and barbed wire and patrolled by unshaven guys with assault rifles and very bad attitudes.

Traveling to Jerusalem from Damascus meant driving into Lebanon's Bekaa Valley past Syrian and Palestinian roadblocks to Beirut, from which, since there are no direct flights between Lebanon and Israel either, we would have to connect through another airport such as Athens or Rome that did offer connections to Tel Aviv. And to end up in Jerusalem, we would have to rent another car.

Armed fanatics made the road from Damascus to Beirut problematic at night. So Roger Matthews, a British friend from the *Financial Times,* and I waited until dawn to set forth in a hired car. I sat in the backseat clutching my birdcage, which drew thigh-slapping jokes in Arabic from burly men who jumped out of the shadows to inspect my passport at one roadblock after another.

At the Beirut airport, we scrambled for the last seats on a flight bound for Rome. By now I was so sick of the birdcage that I wanted to peddle it to some American tourists at the Rome airport who stopped to ask where they could buy one. But there wasn't enough time for a handover because I was racing to catch the final TWA flight to Israel.

Once in Tel Aviv, I had to hitch a ride because all the rental cars had been sucked up by the television networks. After seventeen hours and about twelve hundred miles by air and road, I pulled into Jerusalem with my birdcage.

Though my story of Sadat's speech before the Israeli Knesset led the front page of the *Times,* only two recollections stand out.

One concerned an anorexic blond news poodle who cut in front of me, announcing, "I represent a very important television network." Well, *The New York Times* isn't exactly chopped liver, even if its reporter did come to the biggest story of the year bearing a birdcage.

The other, fonder memory involved the long-distance call I placed to Jaqueline in Cairo, which was historic in being one of the first direct telephone connections between Israel and

Egypt. In Cairo, the phone system was so dismal that I was unable to call Jaqueline from the *Times* bureau downtown, three miles away, to tell her when I would come home. The best chance of making sure that my dinner didn't get fed to Henrietta was to dial home long-distance through Cyprus.

So the Israeli telephone system seemed little short of miraculous. (When I later got stranded in the Sinai desert during a pullback of Israeli forces, an Israeli major pulled a handset from his armored half-track, dialed our Jerusalem bureau, and handed me the telephone to convey my regrets, via Jerusalem and New York, that I would not be back in time to accept a dinner invitation from the American ambassador in Cairo.)

I put my call through to Jaqueline with the cooperation of excited Israeli and Egyptian telephone operators. They were so thrilled to exchange pleasantries with each other that I had to break in to remind them that I really did want to talk to my wife.

"You'll never guess who's here," Jaqueline said when I finally got through. "Henrietta."

"She can't be," I said. It was unlike my wife to play cruel jokes.

"She is." Jaqueline sounded about to dissolve into tears. But the relief in her voice was palpable as she related what now seemed like the children's answered prayers.

She had driven Celia and Chris back from school the previous evening. As they walked toward the apartment entrance, Jaqueline thought she heard a distinctive Siamese twang from behind a palm tree. It was so faint that she stopped in the jasmine-scented darkness to listen.

"Henrietta?" she called

Again there came the same plaintive mewing.

"Henrietta." It was no longer a question.

The cat that hesitantly emerged from the shadows in the jasmine-scented evening was mostly skin and bones, but it was indeed Henrietta.

Her fur was mangy and matted with filth, Jaqueline told me later. But the cat was alive, more than a month after we had given up hope.

When I finally arrived back home after carrying the children's birdcage through six countries in as many days. Jaqueline kissed me at the door.

"We watched you at the news conference on TV," she said. "You were chewing gum when you asked the Israeli prime minister that long question. It looked awful."

I could picture Jaqueline clapping her hands over the children's eyes to spare them the shock. I almost never chew gum unless I've been sent to cover strategic arms negotiations or regional peace talks, where the mutual recriminations drone on for so long that what you really need to bring with your notebook is a bounteous picnic lunch, preferably with a fresh young Beaujolais tucked under the checkered napkin.

My wife is nothing if not well bred, so I promised to park the chewing gum behind my ear if a very important television network should ever be careless enough to offer me big bucks to interview heads of government on camera.

"Where's Henrietta?" I asked.

"Hiding," Jaqueline said. "I still can't believe she's back."

Celia and Chris ran in to hug me, and I presented them with the birdcage. Normally it would have delighted them, but its significance was already eclipsed by the prodigal cat who had finally returned. We never did buy any birds, and the birdcage now hangs in our apartment kitchen in New York, where we keep meaning to stuff it with ferns.

"Want to see where Henrietta is?" Chris asked with a proud smile.

He and Celia took my hands, and together we scampered down the hallway to Chris's room, where I saw nothing at first. Then I spied a cat-sized mound quivering under the white spread covering his bed. I did not try to disturb her.

Henrietta had burrowed down under the blankets of Chris's bed and found refuge in the safest place she knew.

Because Henrietta never confided to me about her ordeal, I can only speculate how she survived, based upon the scars she carried and the quite incredible odds she faced. So let's walk the cat back, to borrow a cliché from the CIA lexicon, and try to re-create what happened.

While a temporary baby-sitter was holding the door open to chat with the neighbors, Henrietta had wandered out of our apartment, down the stairs, and probably outside. That much we already knew.

And when she had tried to come home, she must have confused the apartment on the floor below for ours. Our neighbor downstairs mistook her for a stray street cat, he admitted later, and shooed her out. Confused about where she belonged or perhaps even distracted by a mouse or a potential predator, Henrietta went out of our building to find somewhere safe to stay.

In hunting for food and evading danger over thousands of years, cats have developed a keen sense of smell that is far superior to our own. If even our noses felt assaulted by the exotic fragrances of Cairo, you can imagine how confused Henrietta must have been by these strange pungent, fragrant, rancid odors of the Middle East. There was nothing familiar here to guide her home. She might as well have wandered to the dark side of the moon, which made it all the more incredible that she materialized outside our building nearly a month after she vanished.

Zamalek, where we lived when she disappeared, sits in the middle of the Nile, a lush but congested island (*gezira* in Arabic) surrounded by an overcrowded metropolis, not unlike Manhattan in New York City. Henrietta would have found it hard to leave the island, which is three miles long and a half mile wide, because of the frightening traffic that pounds across the two major bridges.

Zamalek has some dwindling green space in the form of a racetrack and a couple of decaying sporting clubs, but little of its old serenity is left for man or beast. There is some tangled undergrowth to hide in but no shortage of natural enemies for a cat. Feral dogs, gaunt and skittish, harass even the human residents. One such pack attacked me while I was jogging, and I had to fend them off with a plank. There were also plenty of alley cats to challenge Henrietta. Our cat could have survived only by scavenging from the fly-infested piles of garbage rotting in the sun.

As I said earlier, I had hoped that Henrietta would be taken in by some other family. But she returned to us wearing her collar with our Moscow address, which any new owner would have removed. This meant that she had had little choice but to live wild—and had, judging by the cuts and scabs that could have come only from fights with other animals that were just as hungry as she.

Even Cairo's notoriously brazen rats, scurrying up from the murky Nile, would have forced Henrietta to fight or be eaten. The Egyptian rats I've seen came in two sizes: nearly as large as Henrietta and even larger.

As for their prevalence, let me relate an epic battle between man and rat that occurred some years later at the San Stefano, a decaying landmark hotel on the Mediterranean waterfront of Alexandria. The glittering heyday of the San Stefano had long since faded when we stayed there during a visit a few months after Henrietta's miraculous return in Cairo. The odd rat that I glimpsed around the San Stefano looked no more formidable than what I had seen back in Zamalek.

But when workmen were eventually sent to demolish the San Stefano, according to Agence France-Presse, they were chased away by hundreds of fierce rats residing inside the grand old hotel. The workers refused to go back, bringing the demolition to a halt, until Alexandria's health authorities emptied the hotel of its rodent population by lacing the premises with poison.

Henrietta may also have had stones hurled at her by street children or been threatened in other ways, because she was terrified enough by the sound of Arabic to dart back under our son's sheets when we had Egyptian visitors. Our housekeeper, Hassan, gently made Chris's bed over the cat each morning.

The landlord never did get around to making our Zamalek apartment habitable, so we unloaded it on the U.S. Embassy and moved out. Who else would reward a landlord who defaults on his promises by pumping in American tax dollars to do the repairs, then fork out the exorbitant rent? I couldn't complain, and the embassy did need housing for its expanding diplomatic staff.

Before Henrietta returned, we had already decided to relocate across the Nile to a new high-rise apartment building in Giza, a Cairo suburb best known for the Pyramids and the

Sphinx on its western outskirts. If Henrietta had stayed missing for a few more weeks, we would never have found each other.

On the other hand, Henrietta might not have wanted to come back if she had gotten lost a century and a half ago, because under the Ottoman Empire, there was such a thing as a free lunch for stray cats in Cairo. We have the word of Edward William Lane, an Englishman fluent in Arabic who lived in Egypt in the early nineteenth century. His observations are as insightful as those of Alexis de Tocqueville, the French count who toured the United States during the same period.

Lane wrote in his *Manners and Customs of the Modern Egyptians,* first published in London in 1836:

> It is a curious fact that in Cairo houseless cats are fed at the expense of the Kadee (chief judge), or rather almost wholly at his expense. Every afternoon a quantity of offal is brought into the great court before the Mahkem'eh (place of judgment), and the cats are called together to eat.

It seems that a wealthy sultan named Ez-Zahir Beybars bequeathed a garden near his mosque, called Gheyt el-Kuttah, or the cat's garden, the rental income from which was to be used to maintain destitute cats. By the time Lane arrived in Egypt, the garden's annual income had dwindled to fifteen piasters (a few pennies today), so the burden of feeding so many cats fell on the kadee, who was ex officio guardian of all charitable and pious legacies.

"Latterly, however, the duty of feeding the cats has been very inadequately performed," Lane reported. "Many persons in Cairo, when they wish to get rid of a cat, send or take it to the Kadee's house, and let it loose in the great court."

By the time Henrietta arrived in Cairo, there was no more free offal, which was a pity because our cat especially liked liver, kidneys, and other entrails, unless there was some Russian caviar around.

Egypt's hospitality to cats seemed to be rooted in its Islamic as well as pharaonic traditions. One of Celia's best friends, when we lived in Moscow, had been the Malaysian ambassador's daughter Selina. She loved coming to our apartment to play with Henrietta and confided to Celia that she was happy we didn't own a dog as some Western families did.

If a dog touched her, Selina said, she would have to go immediately to wash her hands with sand. Celia was puzzled by this. When we checked further, we realized that Selina's family was Muslim, and the Koran, the holy book of Islam, regards cats as clean but dogs as unclean.

In Cairo, some of our Muslim friends who met Henrietta told us that the prophet Mohammed himself had had a pet cat named Muezza, to whom he had been devoted.

According to a widely told tale, Mohammed once wanted to go outside and pray but found Muezza asleep on his robe. Rather than disturb the cat, the prophet cut off the sleeve of his garment and then slipped away. Another story says that Muezza later repaid the kindness by discovering a snake coiled inside Mohammed's robe and catching it before the serpent could harm her owner.

Sometimes at night, Henrietta would sit on the balcony of our new apartment overlooking the Nile and wail loudly enough to wake up most of Cairo. Once I satisfied myself that she was not being besieged by rats, I assumed that the howling must be her way of working through her nightmare of having been lost. We later discovered that making a nocturnal racket is not unusual behavior for a Siamese cat.

Celia's bedroom was closest to the din, and she sometimes hopped out of bed to make sure that Henrietta was all right but then had trouble going back to sleep. One morning, Celia, who was then about twelve, filed a complaint with us—in Latin, the defunct tongue in which Jaqueline had begun tutoring her.

So let's put a halt to the canard that the younger generation no longer wants to converse in Latin. Here is Celia's after-action report, accompanied by my own imprecise translation, which I trust Latin-savvy readers can improve upon:

Erat nox. Celia in cubiculo dormiebat. Felis ululavit.

(It was night. Celia was sleeping in her room. The cat was howling.)

Celia: Hercle! Cur tu clamorem facis, Henrietta?

(*Celia:* By Hercules! Why are you making noise, Henrietta?)

Felis ululavit. Celia sollicitus erat.

(The cat howled. Celia was concerned.)

Felis ululavit.

(The cat howled.)

Celia: Ego rem intellego. Felis clamorem facis quod omnes dormant. Villa deserta est. Ecce! Ego non dormit, Henrietta, quod tu clamorem mirabilem facis.

(*Celia:* I'm no dummy. The cat is making noise because everyone is sleeping. The house is deserted. Look! I am not sleeping, Henrietta, because you are making one heck of a noise.)

During the day, Henrietta took to sitting on the airy balcony, watching the stubby wooden boats called feluccas tack gracefully across the wide river, catching the desert wind in their billowing white sails.

She sat as silently as Bast, the cat goddess revered by ancient Egyptians, whose statues sometimes depict her in the company of her pharaonic fan, Amenemet I, much as some politicians in the United States pose for photos with activists who park "Reverend" in front of their names.

Jaqueline found Henrietta's resemblance to Bast so remarkable that she went to a museum shop in Cairo and returned with a cobalt-blue replica of the cat goddess. Henrietta found this not at all interesting. She sniffed at the blue statue and went away, offended at being compared with a concrete fake.

Henrietta doubtless felt ambivalent about the pharaohs after she heard about a necropolis at Bubastis that had a separate cemetery for cats. Whether the cats there had been mummified with their consent is one of those trifling details lost to antiquity.

The care with which the ancient Egyptians embalmed their cats seems endearing at first, until you learn that many of the mummified cats were found with their necks broken. This prompted speculation that they had been bred for cushy but short-lived careers as sacrificial victims, not unlike Aztec virgins or some Hollywood starlets.

So many thousands of mummified cats were excavated in Egypt a century ago that their carcasses were eventually shipped in bulk to Europe to be sold as fertilizer for about ten dollars a ton, which was a bargain even in the late nineteenth century.

Of course, mummified crocodiles also turned up in Egypt, proving the existence of a civilization happy to embalm just about anything.

Once her confidence returned, Henrietta grew bored and her urge to explore returned. When workmen came to our apartment to perform the constant repairs, Jaqueline tried to shut Henrietta in the bathroom, whose door opened and closed with a long European handle instead of a round knob. It did not take long for Henrietta to teach herself to jump up on the handle and spring the door ajar with the sheer force of her pounce.

In time she developed a heart-stopping version of her tightrope act, stepping gingerly out to the reinforcing ledge of concrete barely a foot wide that girdled the building. Ignoring the children's pleas to come back, Henrietta fine-tuned her balance with a periodic sweep of her tail as she sauntered along the beam, circling the entire building a harrowing fifteen stories above the Nile riverfront.

Her airy promenade rewarded her with spectacular views. Across the Nile to the east lay downtown Cairo with its exquisite minarets and domes. Beyond was the City of the Dead, a necropolis filled with mausoleums where some Cairenes actually lived, the tombs of the caliphs and the Mamalukes in the Mokattam Hills, and the Khan al-Khalili Bazaar. At the bazaar, we had bought a pair of rugged camel saddles left over from the Egyptian Army's demobilization of its last camel cavalry squadron. As footstools, they made a favorite napping place for Henrietta.

With one paw positioned confidently in front of the other on the narrow concrete beam, she would amble north toward Zamalek, which had once terrified her but now lay submissively at her feet. On the Nile's eastern bank, the Nile Hilton Hotel blocked a decent view of the Egyptian Museum, and on the northern horizon the fertile Nile Delta spread before her like an emerald-colored fan.

Once she turned the corner, Henrietta spied to the west the three pyramids of Giza beyond the canals and fringes of date palms and, had she looked harder, the Sphinx, which would have been awesome had the sculptors finished it off with a cat's ears and whiskers in lieu of the pharaonic head.

Continuing southward, Henrietta could pause to watch camels, their flanks splashed with the executioner's purple dye, plod in procession across the El-Gamaa bridge to the abattoir on the other side of the Nile and, in the distance, more pyramids at Saqqara and the factory smokestacks of Heliopolis.

Finally, calculating the final distance to be covered as carefully as any Flying Wallenda, Henrietta would leap across the void back into our apartment through an open balcony door. And there a relieved Celia and Chris would pour her a bowl of water buffalo milk, delivered to our back door by an smiling vendor in a gownlike galabiya.

In Cairo, Chris resolved to train Henrietta to come when he whistled. Celia scoffed at his naïveté, pointing out the well-known fact that cats could not be taught to respond to human commands as dogs did.

Chris was undeterred. He laid out a messy trail of cat tidbits, this time imported from Italy, from the kitchen into the bedroom, whistling all the while. Predictably, Henrietta followed the tidbits into the bedroom.

"It will never work," Celia reminded him in her big-sister voice.

Next, Chris, again whistling, pulled a string, which Henrietta pounced upon, from one room to the next.

Finally, Chris just whistled and Henrietta appeared, whether out of curiosity or expectation I can't say.

Celia was aghast at this breakthrough. "Everyone knows that you can't train a cat to come when you call," she said.

But thereafter, Henrietta showed up whenever Chris whistled.

Encouraged by this, Chris tried teaching Henrietta more complex tricks, such as sitting on a stool and jumping through a hoop on command. But Henrietta had no interest in becoming a circus performer, and Chris finally gave up.

One Saturday morning, Hassan, our housekeeper, arrived with a smile and a large bag, from which he pulled a set of long, furry ears attached to a small black-and-white rabbit. Celia and Chris clapped with delight, viewing the cuddly rabbit as a perfect playmate for Henrietta as well as themselves.

But Henrietta just stared at the rabbit, which Hassan was dangling by the ears, not knowing quite what to make of the visitor. Our cat, I realized, had never seen a rabbit before. I didn't know how this new arrangement would work out after Henrietta began to gargle her hunting growl.

"Can we keep the bunny rabbit?" Chris begged.

I promised to think about it, which our children knew by then was not much of an answer. But we had reserved some horses at a Bedouin stable near the Pyramids to go riding in the desert and were running late. In Arabic as limited as Hassan's English, I thanked him for the gift and gestured for him to take care of the rabbit until we returned. Hassan nodded eagerly. I pointed to my watch, telling him that we would be back by one o'clock, in time for lunch.

During our drive out to the Pyramids, Celia and Chris discussed what to call Henrietta's new playmate and where to bed it down. I told them that a rabbit could be housebroken but I didn't know how to go about it. Such sanitary duties were instinctive for cats.

And speaking of natural instincts, I pointed out that cats traditionally regarded rabbits and other small furry creatures as prey, so we would have to consider Henrietta's feelings. Celia and Chris groaned when I proposed that we wait and see.

The Sahara can get cold in winter, so our horseback ride left us chilled. We returned to our apartment eager for a hot lunch, which Hassan served immediately: fricassee of chicken over rice, with vegetables cooked to a mush, the way Egyptians like them. This is not a cuisine known for stir-frying. The children asked about their bunny, but I said there would be plenty of time to play after lunch.

I heaped out four steaming portions, and we dug in. The fricassee tasted delicious, made from quite the plumpest chicken that we had eaten in Egypt, which tended to produce sinewy birds more appropriate for cockfighting.

Alerted by the aroma, Henrietta trotted in. Jaqueline prepared a small plate for her and set it on the floor. Henrietta cleaned her plate and mewed eagerly for more.

Slowly, the reality dawned on me. The children's new rabbit, or a portion of it, was steaming on the end of my fork.

We adults might have gotten away with it had not Hassan walked in, beaming, to take credit for the meal.

"Kwais?" he asked in Arabic. Good?

"Where's our bunny rabbit?" Chris asked him.

Hassan pointed proudly to the casserole. *"Kwais?"* he repeated, beaming.

Celia burst into tears. She dropped her fork, to which bits

of bunny were still attached, and ran sobbing to her bedroom.

Chris's jaw dropped. He threw me a look of utter betrayal and took off too.

Jaqueline was sufficiently upset to declare that she wasn't hungry either, having galloped only halfway across the Sahara that morning. She too left me at the table and went off to console the children.

That left me sitting alone, wondering about the propriety of finishing a delicious meal. Henrietta, smacking her chops, displayed no such pangs of conscience.

More, she mewed. More.

"Kwais awi," I told Hassan. Very good. And please, I added, don't serve the family rabbit again.

We had lived abroad long enough that we no longer expected our food to come shrink-wrapped in packages from the supermarket. But it is one thing to eat rabbit for dinner and quite another to introduce it to your kids first and imagine a name before it is slaughtered, skinned, and popped into the skillet.

There is no point in dwelling upon what had become a bad hare day for the Wren family, if you'll excuse the pun, but I wondered whether Henrietta might have put Hassan up to it. She had succeeded in eliminating a rival without having to do the messy killing and eviscerating herself. She dined well on the leftover rabbit that the rest of us could not quite bring ourselves to eat.

In time Henrietta also began eating carrots, which our cook prepared with rice and fresh fish from the Nile. But this nourishing concoction never dampened the appetite of her inner carnivore. Our cat would never pass up a choice cut of meat.

During the peak of Cairo's sweltering summers, when the temperature soared to the triple digits, Jaqueline would take Celia and Chris back to New York to visit their grandparents and have annual checkups by their pediatrician and dentist. If I wasn't traveling elsewhere in the Middle East, I reported from Cairo, returning each evening to Henrietta, buoyed by the thought of the imported shell steaks that Jaqueline had hoarded for me in the freezer.

This was no small feat because except for the odd water buffalo and sheep, the government had temporarily banned the sale of choicer cuts of meat from European cattle, as part of an economic austerity drive that fizzled out a few months later.

As soon as I got home to our apartment in Giza, I turned the air conditioners on full blast and fed Henrietta her Nile fish prepared with carrots and rice. Then I showered and cooked a steak for myself, figuring that our cat, having just been fed, wouldn't pester me for a piece. I usually passed up eating lunch in hot weather, so by evening I was hungry.

It did not take many such nights to find myself down to the tenderest, juiciest-looking steak, which I had saved for last. That evening, I flipped the sizzling steak, medium rare, out of the skillet and onto my plate. I popped the cap off an ice-cold bottle of Stella beer, a weak Egyptian pilsner that made up in thirst-slaking quantity what it lacked in body or taste, when the telephone rang.

A copy editor was calling from New York to suggest some cuts in an article that would be published tomorrow.

Line by line, I negotiated the trims in my story, oblivious to the aromatic sizzle of the steak that I'd left sitting on the dining-room table.

After I finished with the copy editor, I hung up and returned to the dining room, where I was met by a horrifying sight: Henrietta was gobbling up my steak.

To be fair to our cat, she did not devour the entire steak. But she had pretty well chewed it into shreds until it looked as ravaged as the carcass of an antelope disemboweled by a pride of lions.

My screams alerted her to this violation of our primal compact, which had never included my steak. Henrietta must have realized that her behavior was impermissible, because she abandoned the shredded meat and jumped off the table.

There followed some high-impact aerobics called Chase-the-Cat-with-the-Broom until I gave up the romp around our apartment and retired, meatless, to bed.

My aerobics partner elected to spend the night as far under the living-room sofa as she could crawl.

But Henrietta was guilty of nothing more than acting like a cat. If you were descended from a long and distinguished line of carnivores, would you settle for fish boiled with carrots and rice if you smelled a steak sizzling in the next room?

It would please me to report that I immediately forgave our cat for indulging her most natural urge. The truth is that I didn't, at least not that night.

As our posting in Cairo approached the end of its third year, the *Times* flew me back to headquarters to discuss the next assignment. It was late August, and I had been shuttling between Egypt and Israel. Jaqueline was already in New York with Celia and Chris for their annual appointments with the dentist and pediatrician.

It didn't seem worth putting Henrietta through the expense and upheaval of another overseas journey if we would be back in Cairo after a couple weeks. Our housekeeper, Hassan, had gone to his village in upper Egypt, so I instructed his successor on taking care of the cat while we were gone.

In New York, I was thrilled to be told that I would become bureau chief in Beijing, the assignment I had requested. The *Times* even agreed to send me first to an intensive Chinese language program at Cambridge University that at the time was used to prepare British diplomats bound for China.

After seven years of hardship posts in Moscow and Cairo, Jaqueline looked forward to living in England again, if only for a while. In the two years she had spent studying at Oxford University, she had acquired, besides a master's degree with honors—honours?—an Anglophilia suffused with the passion that you would normally expect from a New York Yankees fan in the final innings of the World Series.

We all flew back to Cairo via London, where we visited Cambridge to rent a house and find schools for Celia and Chris. I enrolled in the Chinese Language Project, as the Cambridge course was called.

But our enthusiasm subsided once we gave belated thought to Henrietta, whose welfare now posed a potential obstacle to our plans for a tidy sabbatical at Cambridge.

Britain's stringent regulations required that any pet brought into the country first spend six months in quarantine, to prevent it from carrying in rabies.

The British government has lately relaxed its restriction to admit pets from other European countries, provided that they have recently been vaccinated against rabies and have a microchip implanted under their skin for identification. But Henrietta wouldn't have qualified under the new rules because she would have come from the Middle East, where rabies is a problem.

My Chinese course was scheduled to last about forty weeks, so we calculated that Henrietta could join us for the final four months after she was paroled, giving her the opportunity to sample the delights of an English summer.

But it was hard to think of storing a cherished member of the family in a cage down in London from autumn into spring.

Our misgivings about quarantine grew once we returned to Cairo and found that Henrietta had visibly deteriorated during our relatively brief absence.

She watched our arrival with eyes marred by what looked like a greasy film clouding part of her vision. What I mistook at first for cataracts turned out to be swollen haws, the nictitating membranes that cats and some other animals possess to draw over their corneas like a spare protective eyelid when their senses are dulled by malnutrition, a virus, or generally poor health.

It was clear that something was wrong when Henrietta did not bestir herself to give Celia and Chris her usual greeting. Instead of rubbing against them and rolling over to have her belly stroked, Henrietta responded to their petting by listlessly lowering her small head and closing her rheumy eyes, as though life had finally defeated her.

This was not the spunky cat we all knew. We conjectured that Henrietta must have been fed poorly while we were away. Or maybe she had simply despaired of ever seeing us again. Our new housekeeper professed ignorance of Henrietta's decline.

With a healthy new diet, some vitamin supplements, and unstinting affection from Celia and Chris, Henrietta's eyes cleared up, and within a few weeks she returned to her old self.

Chris had come back from England bearing a stuffed toy

mouse covered with fake fur, which he had named Woodstock for the town where he had bought it. Henrietta, as the family authority on mice, liberated Woodstock for herself. She pried open Chris's chest of drawers, another skill she had acquired, and abducted the lifelike rodent, which did not last long under her care. Henrietta liked to lie on her back with Woodstock between her claws while she gnawed merrily on its head.

A mouse was a mouse was a mouse, as far as our cat was concerned. Two other toy mice, named Prestbury and Cheltenham for the English towns where Chris collected them, fared no better once Henrietta turned her attention to them.

In the back of all our minds lay the hope of postponing Henrietta's separation from her family for as long as possible, now that she had only just recovered from her illness. Celia and Chris were still enrolled for another term at the British school in Cairo, so Jaqueline, much as she wanted to go to England, proposed staying with them until the end of the year.

We agreed that I would proceed alone to Cambridge to start studying Chinese and return to Cairo over Christmas vacation to collect the family and move us all to England.

But this posed new problems for consigning Henrietta to the mandatory six months of British quarantine, because she would be discharged barely a month before we expected to leave England for China. Though I did not say so, I was worried about whether Henrietta, having fought to survive on the garbage dumps of Cairo, would have her spirit broken by quarantine in London.

Just as one does not run out on a fellow reporter in distress, I could not easily abandon so constant a companion as Henrietta. My plan to spend a year studying in England before going to China left me feeling more than a little selfish.

Contrary to my expectations when I first went overseas, I encountered no shortage of journalists who juggled cat ownership with the chaos of their professional and personal lives.

After Andrew Rosenthal, who at this writing is the *Times* foreign editor, worked in Moscow for the Associated Press, he went through the throes of a divorce, which is not uncommon among foreign correspondents. After he moved to Washington, Andy told me he suspected that his former wife timed his absence on the campaign trail to spirit away Alfie, the cat they had acquired together in Moscow.

And when Steven Weisman was the *Times* bureau chief in New Delhi, his family owned two cats, Zeke and Polly. "It was comforting to have a pet overseas," Steve told me.

One day Zeke, a caramel-colored tomcat, vanished, leaving Steve and his wife, Elisabeth Bumiller, distraught. Whenever Steve saw India's ominous vultures perched in the trees, he found himself imagining the worst possible fate for Zeke. After all, what cat in his right mind would deliberately go out and make himself a moving target for vultures with wingspans the breadth of a Boeing 737's when home offered a tasty daily diet of water buffalo and rice?

But a couple of weeks later, Zeke casually reappeared, much as our own Henrietta had in Cairo, looking more than a little mangy and with no hint as to how he had survived. Edible pickings on the streets in New Delhi for a "billy," as Indians call a cat, were at least as slim as they were in Cairo.

"Zeke, where have you been?" Elisabeth tearfully asked, Steve recalled later.

"He can't speak," their cook, Toheed, interjected. "He's a cat!"

I found myself involved when another *Times* colleague,

John Kifner, had one of his two Siamese cats take leave of his apartment in Beirut. Kif was not in Beirut at the time but in Tehran, where a bunch of Muslim student radicals had overrun the U.S. Embassy, taking its diplomats hostage. The *Times* dispatched me to Tehran to help Kif cover the crisis.

Now, "wimp" is not a word that comes to mind in describing a wisecracking former police reporter like Kif, who was then our Beirut correspondent. As soon as refugees start pouring out of some hot spot, odds are that Kif is rushing in.

Imagine that some obscure country is plunged into revolution and the old dictator tries to flee the successor despot, but his plane crashes on takeoff because it is overloaded with gold bullion looted from the government treasury, and anyhow, everyone is too preoccupied to notice because of a mudslide or tsunami that suddenly swallows the capital.

This sort of thing can occur more often than you might think, and if you're curious about what it portends for American foreign policy, or at least the Dow Jones, Kif is the reporter you would want to sort it all out in two thousand words in time for tomorrow's newspaper.

But even Kif's sangfroid has its limits, which when we worked together in Tehran were his two Siamese cats, a mother and son whom he had affectionately named Studs and Duke.

The timing of Duke's disappearance could not have been worse for a couple of foreign correspondents trying to stave off expulsion from Iran. Rumors persisted of an imminent American raid to free the diplomatic hostages. Soviet troops had already invaded Afghanistan next door, and Kif had just returned from a romp with the Afghan guerrillas.

The story in Tehran had become much too volatile to abandon. The Iranian authorities, unhappy with the negative coverage they were getting, had begun refusing visas to new correspondents, so Kif and I were hanging on in Iran by our fingernails.

Alerted to Kif's family emergency, the deputy foreign editor dispatched the *Times's* Rome correspondent to Beirut to search for the cat. This took a couple of days, by which time Duke had taken up residence in Beirut's back alleys and would not be enticed out by just any stranger.

So we hatched a plan whereby Kif would sneak back into Beirut overnight to retrieve Duke while I continued filing news from Tehran to cover his brief absence. Had Henrietta been missing, Kif doubtless would have done the same for me. Besides, he was confident that he could retrieve his cat in a matter of minutes and be back in Tehran on the next available flight.

Just as predicted, Kif returned to Beirut, whistled Duke out of hiding, and returned him to the apartment in about fifteen minutes. But when Kif stopped by the Iranian Embassy on the way to the airport to pick up a fresh visa, the bearded militant in charge refused to accommodate him.

Kif continued pleading his case in Beirut while I went to the Ministry of National Guidance in Tehran and told the hard-line official who handled our accreditation about Kif's humanitarian mission. Any correspondent with enough heart to take a risk for his cats, I said, could not help but admire the even more glorious sacrifices of the Iranian revolution.

In retrospect, it was a ridiculous non sequitur. But the Iranian hard-liner, who had covered his office walls with photographs of malnourished American Indians to show how much worse things were in the United States, professed to be moved by Kif's efforts on behalf of his cat.

"Then you'll expedite his visa?" I said hopefully.

"No, no," the hard-liner snickered, and dissolved into peals of laughter.

Fortunately, Kif browbeat a visa out of the Iranian chargé d'affaires in Beirut and returned to Tehran in enough time for both of us to get expelled as undesirables with the rest of the American reporters.

The editor never knew of Kif's cat rescue because nobody dared tell him what had happened.

Paris to (Eventually) Tokyo

I went off to Cambridge alone, as Jaqueline and I had agreed, to begin my intensive Chinese study. I returned to Cairo during the university's Christmas vacation to fetch the family, including Henrietta, and pitch in with the final packing.

By now, Jaqueline and I were convinced that Henrietta would fare poorly in British quarantine. No less important, anything that jeopardized our cat's restored health could give the Chinese a reason to refuse to admit her. China, like most other countries, does not want to import sickly animals, even when they're pets.

Fortunately, Jaqueline's mother, Frances Braxton, is a woman who rises admirably to any emergency. She agreed to let Henrietta join her own two cats at her home in Scarsdale, New York, while we were in England. We would collect our cat on the way to Beijing in September.

Yet first Henrietta had to get to New York—alone. Rather than fly directly to London and have to put our cat into quarantine even temporarily, I booked a flight for us to Paris on New Year's Day. There we could put Henrietta on a subsequent flight to New York before continuing on to England ourselves.

But on that final leg across the Atlantic, Henrietta's reservation was made not in the aircraft cabin but in the hold with other air freight. We made her sturdy traveling case as comfortable as possible, putting in a few toys and a familiar small blanket that smelled of our children. Henrietta also needed to bring papers from a veterinarian in Egypt attesting to her good health and showing that her rabies shots were up to date.

On the case's wooden exterior, we taped address labels and telephone numbers and attached copies of Henrietta's health and vaccination records for any customs officials who needed to inspect them.

Celia and Chris, who had been traveling for years on their own passports, once made a tiny passport for Henrietta bound in blue construction paper. They drew some make-believe visas and a clever cartoon of our cat where the photograph should have gone. We stopped producing the cat's passport at customs and immigration after it failed to entertain the inspectors, some of whom suspected a forgery.

We arranged for Henrietta to fly with us to Paris. In the boarding area at Cairo airport, she piqued the curiosity of a group of American tourists who were wrapping up a package tour and heading back home to wherever the inhabitants wear plaid trousers and fanny packs.

What, they wanted to know, was a cat doing traveling around the Middle East?

It was not an unreasonable question in airport departure lounges, where we tried to let Henrietta out of her case for a little exercise. We had fed and watered her well before leaving for the airport. If you were waiting for your flight to be called and discovered a small gray cat poking around your carry-on bag, you would be entitled to know something about the visitor beyond the fact that she wasn't there to sniff out illicit drugs for the customs service.

Occasionally, some tourist, invariably from California, would jump up, scream that she was allergic to cats, and demand that Henrietta be banished from the airport. To be honest, we never paid much notice because in air travel anything goes these days, as you may have noticed from the hairy males who consider tank tops the height of fashion and wind up sweating in the seat next to you.

Henrietta didn't mind the gentle petting of strangers, though when small, hyperactive children lurched for her, she would beat a hasty retreat back into her case.

By now Celia and Chris had grown adept at politely fielding all the questions about Henrietta. But leaving Cairo on this New Year's Day, we all were too exhausted after packing up our household to explain that the cat belonged to a foreign correspondent's family, which invariably set a full colloquy in motion.

It seemed much more polite to fudge.

"Our cat goes on all our holidays," I explained, which was true enough. "She refuses to be left behind."

"How long has she been traveling?" someone asked.

"We left the States last Thursday," I said, "or maybe it was Friday. It's a weekend thing."

"That's got to cost you a bundle," scoffed a man whose own wealth appeared to have been invested in the cameras that hung from his neck.

Here I shrugged. "The money isn't important," I said, implying that enough was left over to pay for our children's visits to the dentist. "It's what our cat discovers about her inner kitten, that's what matters."

The tourists buzzed through the flight over what we'd implied was our extravagant lifestyle.

Flying Air France to Paris felt like the New Year's Eve party that we hadn't found time for the night before. No sooner were the wheels up from Cairo than the flight attendants started pouring free champagne.

Henrietta didn't fancy champagne because of the bubbles.

But she wolfed down the smoked salmon on our lunch trays and licked the salt off whatever fallen cocktail nuts she was able to scavenge under the seats. In a commendable display of laissez-faire, or joie de vivre, or just je ne sais quoi, the Air France flight attendants allowed Henrietta to sit on our laps and wander about the cabin, meowing "Bonjour" to her fellow passengers, including the tour group in the back.

The tough decisions came after we landed at Charles de Gaulle International Airport. Henrietta deserved a night out in Paris, where brasseries, I'm told, have no objection to seeing pets join their owners at the table. The writer Colette offered an insight into Parisian tolerance when she wrote that "by associating with the cat, one only risks becoming richer."

But we didn't want Henrietta's stomach upset by the exquisite mussels or steak tartare before her intercontinental journey. So we took *le chat,* as the French call a cat, to the Air France baggage terminal and checked her on the next flight bound for New York.

However many misgivings we had about checking Henrietta into quarantine in England, shipping her alone across the Atlantic suddenly seemed worse. There's really no way to tell a cat to keep her whiskers up because you'll be seeing her again in seven or eight months. Would she conclude that we had abandoned her forever?

Sensing that the wrenching separation was imminent at last, Henrietta began to moan as the air freight agent weighed and tagged her box with a consoling "*Zut, alors.*"

Nicholas Hayes, an American banker who was our neighbor in Zamalek, had a cat that underwent a nervous breakdown after relocating from Bangkok to Cairo. The cat started losing its fur to the point of going bald until Nick, on the advice of a Cairo veterinarian, administered Valium, a tranquilizer sold without prescription over the counter in local pharmacies. On Valium, Nick's cat stopped shedding and recovered.

Mindful of his cat's experience with jet travel, Jaqueline rummaged through her travel bag of precautionary medications for a bit of Valium to soothe Henrietta's nerves. It was, after all, the first time our cat would cross the ocean without us. As Celia later observed, it felt to us like packing a child in a box.

At last Jaqueline found the traveling vial of Valium, broke apart a five-milligram tablet, and forced a piece of it through Henrietta's teeth. But *le chat* looked so inconsolable that Jaqueline relented and gave her the rest of the tablet.

Wailing a wrenching "*Au revoir, ma famille*" piteously enough to seize up our throats, Henrietta disappeared down the conveyor belt and into the bowels of the freight terminal.

Even an eight-hour flight in the hold of a Boeing 747 was preferable for Henrietta to six months of quarantine at Heathrow, we assured the children during the taxi ride into Paris.

After we checked in to our small hotel off the rue Scribe, I called Stephen Jessel, a Paris-based correspondent for the British Broadcasting Corporation who was studying Chinese with me at Cambridge in preparation for his own posting to Beijing. Stephen and his wife, Jane, whisked us off to an elegant brasserie that I doubt would have opened its menu to Henrietta.

But Jaqueline began to worry that she had miscalculated Henrietta's dosage. Five milligrams of Valium would knock me out for the night, and Jaqueline decided that it was much too much for an eight-pound cat.

Back at our hotel, Jaqueline placed a long-distance call through the hotel operator to her mother in Scarsdale, who asked the American Society for Prevention of Cruelty to Animals about the potential effect. Whoever answered helpfully said that our cat would be dead on arrival at Kennedy International Airport from a drug overdose.

Jaqueline called her sister, Merwin, in New York City. Our hotel phone bill was inflating nearly as fast as a bill at a three-star restaurant in the *Guide Michelin*.

Merwin raced out to Kennedy that night with a couple of her children in tow to locate Henrietta and attempt to administer whatever emergency resuscitation was needed. When the cat's box was dumped in the baggage claim area, my sister-in-law, expecting the worst, retrieved it and opened the door.

Thereupon emerged Henrietta, a bit wobbly on her feet, certainly, but hardly the worse for wear. If anything, her condition could be described as mellow.

Once Jaqueline learned the good news of Henrietta's safe arrival, we all slept better. A day later, we flew on to England, still feeling the absence of our family member.

Some people would call spending a year at Cambridge University a boondoggle. And so it was, if you exclude the inconvenience of having to memorize 2,600 Chinese characters, pronounce them pitch perfect, and write them down in proper order of pen strokes.

I grappled with the four tones of spoken Chinese by assigning a different color to each inflection. Though my Chinese has since deteriorated badly, when I close my eyes and think of Shanghai, I still see blue and red and pronounce it in the fourth and third tones. When I see an American cat, or *meiguo mao,* I think red-green-black, for third, second, and first tones, though at Cambridge I envisioned gray too, for our absent Henrietta.

I copied each character in its designated color on a small card to carry around. Jaqueline objected when she caught me shuffling through a handful of the cards during the evensong service at King's College Chapel.

Our rented house overlooked the river Cam and Midsummer Common, a grassy expanse that sparkled with the morning dew. Our home resonated with the sounds of Chinese language tapes that recycled themselves through my brain at night.

We bicycled everywhere, Chris to King's College School (whose choirboys sing the celebrated Christmas service of lessons and carols), Celia to the Perse School for Girls, and Jaqueline and I to our respective classes at Cambridge.

But something was missing when I walked or pedaled through the old university town and saw plump cats napping in the cottage windows or sitting in the gardens soaking up the winter sunlight. Henrietta would have fitted in there.

On the other hand, after watching the undergraduates careening about on bicycles, I was surprised not to find more of Cambridge's sleek cats transmogrified into roadkill.

Jaqueline's father died while we were in Cambridge, and she flew back to New York. She returned with other unsettling news: despite the good care, Henrietta was homesick for us. She showed no interest in my mother-in-law's two cats. Our cat climbed into a box on a kitchen shelf and spent her days sleeping curled up under the fluorescent light, descending only to eat sparingly or use the litter box.

I had heard plenty of stories about faithful dogs that pined away for their masters, but it had never occurred to me that cats, with their show of independence, would develop similarly deep attachments. Jaqueline reported upon her return that Henrietta was inconsolable without our children and felt abandoned.

In August, Jaqueline again left for New York, this time with

Celia and Chris. I finished my Chinese course and took over the last of the packing. It was another of those complex moves, with some of our things airfreighted to Beijing, others traveling by sea to Hong Kong, and the rest shipped to the United States for storage. We're still not sure where everything went, especially a brass samovar I had acquired in Kiev, which, according to the waybill, continues to circle the globe aboard an Iran Air flight.

By the time I arrived, Jaqueline and the children had collected Henrietta from Scarsdale. Our cat looked sick and aged, though she was not yet ten years old. But after a few nights spent sleeping on our children's beds, Henrietta miraculously perked up and began to act like her old self again.

We had underestimated Henrietta's appetite for travel. Once on the road with us again, she thrived.

I initially bought into the misconception that a cat's intelligence could be measured by the extent to which it agreed to subordinate its interests to those of its mistress or master.

But Henrietta refused to perch obediently on my safari jacket like some pirate's parrot or to view the world from the security of Jaqueline's shoulder bag. When adventure presented itself, Henrietta pushed the envelope. Once in motion, our cat could cover more territory than a cross-eyed bird dog, sometimes without ever leaving the airport.

During one of our departures from Kennedy International Airport, an officious fellow presiding over the metal detector at the security checkpoint insisted on physically inspecting the interior of Henrietta's travel cage, which at the time was tagged, I recall, as cabin luggage for Cairo.

"Open the box," he demanded.

"That's not a good idea," I demurred. "It's just a cat and a blanket in there, as anyone can see."

This infuriated him. Ignoring my warning, he grabbed the cage away from me and flung the door open.

Henrietta went ballistic, hurtling past him with nearly the velocity of a cruise missile. In the confusion that ensued, it took us all some time to find her. At length I spied Henrietta, not cowering in a cranny of the bustling departure terminal but brazenly lining up to board some other airliner to Copenhagen, having doubtless checked out the destinations available on the board of departing flights. Even if she hadn't chosen the foreign correspondent's life, this cat was born to travel.

By now Henrietta had made herself so indispensible to our itinerant lifestyle that Celia, who was about to turn fourteen, captured the relationship in a poem. Here are a couple of her verses:

The Wrens, they love to travel,
It's the thing they love to do.
They love to stand in airport lines
To get their luggage through.
They love to visit foreign lands,
To them it's just a game,
And to visit every airport
Is their one ultimate aim.

Whenever the Wrens travel
They always travel light,
Twenty suitcases or so
On every single flight.
To top it off, a Siamese cat

Who wants to have her say,
And that's the sort of commonplace thing
The Wrens do every day.

Henrietta came to alert us to which airlines offer true hospitality, something that has influenced my choice of carrier to this day.

Air France and Portugal's TAP were certainly the cat-friendliest. This may be because the French and Portuguese aren't hung up about letting pets into their cafés and restaurants either, as we Anglo-Saxons are.

British Airways banned cats in its cabins. An Englishman dotes upon his cat if it's British but deems a cat of any other nationality deserving of penal isolation, not unlike the early convicts transported to Australia. To be fair, I must add that British Airways brews a terrific cup of tea.

Japan Airlines was so unfailingly polite about having our cat on board that it seemed rude to inquire about what its rules actually were.

Most American airlines were willing to carry our cat in the cabin if we booked her sufficiently in advance, to avoid the prospect of dueling felines aboard.

Lufthansa ordered our cat directly into the hold.

When it came to air travel, being treated like a cat galled Henrietta because, as Celia kept reminding us, our cat no longer thought of herself as one. Having groused about the appalling conditions in the hold after her first transcontinental flight on British Airways, Henrietta made us devise strategems for taking her out of her case once we were aboard.

She would lie motionless under a blanket on Celia's or Chris's lap during takeoffs and landings. When airborne, her restraint invariably yielded to curiosity. She sallied forth to stalk imaginary mice under the rows of seats, slinking past the legs of other passengers, most of whom seemed delighted to encounter her. Others may have been less amused, but I cannot recall that any flight attendants complained about a cat running loose under the seats.

But when we flew to Beijing, Henrietta went too far on the segment from Los Angeles to Tokyo.

We had stopped briefly in California to visit my mother in suburban Woodland Hills. Henrietta held a staring contest with her reflection in the swimming pool at the Holiday Inn but stopped short of taking a dip in the water.

Once airborne again, Henrietta grew bored somewhere near the international date line. Halfway through the eleven-hour flight over the Pacific, she vaulted over the seat in front of us, landing squarely on the bald head of a dozing Japanese businessman.

He was terribly nice about it, smiling and waving off my apologies, but neither of us went back to sleep.

Thereafter, Henrietta had to endure an in-flight leash, which left her less ambulatory and also tended to wake up other passengers when it entwined around their ankles.

Henrietta enjoyed Japan at first sniff. On our taxi ride into Tokyo from Narita International Airport, the cool night air was redolent with exotic odors that hinted at adventures to come and revived the cat after her longest intercontinental flight.

After spending a few minutes flirting with her first taxi driver in Asia, Henrietta rose on her hind legs and pressed her whiskers against the partly lowered window to breathe in the unfamiliar fragrances of Tokyo.

But when we checked into the deluxe Okura Hotel, the

management declined to let Henrietta share our room, which cost well over $300 a night. Instead, the bellhops were ordered to assemble an elaborate zoolike cage in the basement where she had to stay. Her caterwauling and pacing so impressed the hotel bellhops that they nicknamed Henrietta "the puma."

The Okura Hotel's banishment of Henrietta to its spic-and-span dungeon seemed to me a Western corruption of Japanese culture, which has a tradition of giving cats some respect. When a dog chased the cat belonging to one of Japan's early emperors, he had the offending hound packed off to the countryside and its owner put in prison. By contrast, halfway around the world, the Europeans, possessed by a vicious piety, all but exterminated their cats by burning and torturing the helpless creatures under the twisted misconception that they were familiars of the Devil. Europe got what it deserved, which was the rat-borne plague, or Black Death, that wiped out a third of the population.

The comedians Carl Reiner and Mel Brooks, in their take on history, *The 2000 Year Old Man,* summed up the plague as "too many rats, not enough cats."

In Japan, cats were appreciated, especially after they saved Japan's silk industry by scything down the rats who were devouring the commercially valuable silkworm cocoons.

My point in bringing all this up is that Henrietta would have fared better had we arranged her accommodations at one of the temples and monasteries we visited in Tokyo and later in Kyoto, where cats were permitted to lounge about undisturbed. You don't see a lot of that in the great cathedrals of Europe.

We looked in on our *neko,* as a cat is called in Japanese, confined in her spartan cage down in the basement of the Okura Hotel. But we still had to go out and find new underwear for

Chris, whose undershirts and drawers had been left behind on our last continent, in the clothes dryer at his grandmother's house.

In front of some Japanese houses and shops, we saw painted porcelain statuettes of the sitting *maneki neko*—the traditional invitational cat that beckons in friends or customers, depending upon whether its left or right paw is hoisted in greeting. At least, that was how my karate instructor, Isami Shiroma, has explained it, though Isami wasn't quite sure whether a raised left paw signified friendship and a right paw meant commerce or the other way around.

We returned to the five-star Okura Hotel to find our own *maneki neko* beckoning us from her no-star accommodations in the basement. Her wails were audible enough in the glittering lobby to reproach us for having neglected her again. "Is this how you treat your fellow traveler?" she seemed to say.

Some Japanese find it easier to consider life from the cat's perspective. Take, for example, a monologue attributed to the cat who inhabits the title of Natsume Soseki's modern novel *I Am a Cat.* "If we are not careful, even cats might become influenced by this cramped world. That would be terrible," it mused. This prospect so depressed the cat that it slunk off to sneak a drink from its master's beer barrel, tumbled in, and drowned. Soseki's novel, never a contender for the *Cat-in-the-Hat* category of happy children's literature, does raise some credibility problems for those of us who have taken our cats to Japan and never seen them choose a bottle of Asahi beer over a bland saucer of milk.

The staff at the Okura Hotel smiled and fussed over our departure, though I suspect they were no sorrier to see Henrietta go than she was to check out of her basement cage. She put her paw down firmly and refused to stay in any more hotels that offered accommodations behind metal bars. On occasion we found ourselves taking Henrietta into hotels without burdening the staff with formal registration.

And I must say that she did her part to earn better treatment, because she behaved far more graciously as a hotel guest than what I've heard about the Rolling Stones on tour. She never threw a tantrum over the bowl, cat food, and folding litter box that Jaqueline produced from our luggage. We set up her box in the bathtub between showers, and Henrietta discreetly absented herself whenever the maid came to clean the room.

With Henrietta's reproaches ringing in our ears, we ended our stay in Tokyo and headed for her next country, China.

Beijing

Just as some Westerners navigate by the astrological signs of the zodiac—I'm a Pisces, since you've asked—the Chinese look to their own twelve birth signs, as measured out in successive lunar years of the rat, ox, tiger, rabbit, dragon, snake, horse, sheep, monkey, rooster, dog, and pig.

By my calculation, Henrietta was actually born under the sign of the rat, but it seemed much more fitting to place her with the rest of her species under the tiger's sign. Moreover, she demonstrated some traits attributed to those born in the Year of the Tiger. I'll concede that our cat could hardly be called (a) powerful or (b) aggressive, but she was (c) brave and (d) adventurous. At the same time, Henrietta possessed other virtues attributed to those born in the Year of the Rat, being (e) observant, (f) diligent, and (g) quick, though not particularly (h) thrifty.

So the omens for Henrietta's good fortune in China looked promising when we arrived in Beijing on a sunny October day. We drove down the capital's broad thoroughfare, Changan Boulevard, to the Beijing Hotel, where we lived until a *Times* apartment became available a couple of weeks later in a compound newly built for foreigners.

The compound's Chinese name, Jianguomenwai, means "Outside the Establish-the-State Gate," though the actual imperial gate was demolished after the Communists took power in 1949. The rows of concrete high-rise buildings along Changan today exemplify some of the worst architecture conceived under socialism—and the competition has been stiff. I can envision Chinese delegates boasting at some proletarian conference on Really Dreadful Communist Architecture, "You think Pyongyang and Ulan Bator are eyesores? Come see how we've ruined our capital."

Fortunately, the eloquent place names have survived around Beijing, unlike in Moscow, where everything was renamed after the winners in the 1917 Bolshevik Revolution and changed back again after the Soviet Union fell apart. How could you not be tempted to spend a day goofing off, as many Chinese do, at the old Summer Palace on the outskirts of Beijing if you knew that its quaintly remarkable abodes carry exquisite names such as the Pavilion of Heart Purifying, the Clarity Inviting House, the Hall of Delight and Longevity, or the Court of Virtuous Harmony?

The Summer Palace had a restaurant, Tingli Guan, which translates as the Hall for Listening to Orioles, though I never trusted the fish pulled from the polluted Kunming Lake enough to dine there. Birds figure prominently in Chinese names, but cats don't. If there is a Hall for Listening to Cats Caterwauling, I never found it.

The Beijing Hotel, however, was as billed, a grand if slightly gloomy hotel in Beijing whose high ceilings and carpeted hallways date back to the late Qing Dynasty, which is to say before the imperial Qings were shoved aside in 1911. It must have been about then when our room was last cleaned thoroughly, though no one thought to refer to the Beijing Hotel as the Inn of Tinkling Pipes and Slovenly Service. Some foreign guests did nickname it the Heartbreak Hotel, a reference not to Elvis Presley but to greedy Western businessmen who stayed there, hoping to close lucrative deals with the Chinese only to find themselves outwitted and fleeced by their canny hosts.

"We Have Friends All over the World," a gold-on-red

毛語錄
1
毛語錄
2
毛語錄
3

embroidered screen boasted in Chinese and English near the Beijing Hotel's eastern entrance. I wonder whether such chest-thumping sentiments, which had to include Henrietta, survived the makeover that the Beijing Hotel later underwent to make it look as indistinguishable as possible from every other world-class hotel.

Anyhow, the Virtuous Cat of Insatiable Inquisitiveness—I refer of course to Henrietta—immediately felt at home in the Beijing Hotel, where the chambermaids were invariably busy with group chatfests and ignored her daily patrols down the corridors. So the Feline of Ten Thousand Exquisite Discoveries could pretty much roam wherever she chose, even climbing into the hotel's ersatz Ming Dynasty planters to nibble at the greenery and cough up her hairballs.

And no one complained. Had we paraded a family of aardvarks on leashes across the red carpets of the hotel lobby, the management would have paid us scant attention. The Chinese expected *yang gweidze,* or foreign devils, to behave oddly and, while we lived in Beijing, charged us well for our eccentricities.

The Beijing Hotel had a couple of conspicuous advantages, the first being location-location-location at the prime corner of Changan and Wangfujing, the downtown shopping street. The other was a cavernous dining room that served the capital's best *suan la tang,* or hot-and-sour soup, and did not stint on the spices when it served *gongbao jiding,* or chicken with hot peppers and peanuts.

It was Henrietta's first introduction to Chinese cuisine, and while she found it a little too highly seasoned for her delicate palate, she nuzzled aside the hot peppers and peanuts and lapped up the chicken, which had been diced to just the right size.

While we were living in the Beijing Hotel, Henrietta was summoned to undergo a medical examination pronouncing her fit to live in the People's Republic of China. Our cat's vaccination records had just been updated by a veterinarian in Scarsdale, but this was not enough in Beijing. No, we were told, Henrietta had to be examined by an official Chinese veterinarian.

And to whom must we entrust this mandatory procedure on our cherished pet? Why, the People's Liberation Army, of course.

We had little choice but to use an army veterinarian who was accustomed to working on larger draft animals. The civilian veterinarians had been assigned to the countryside, because that was where the livestock lived. The notion that a vet could contribute to the building of a new China by hanging around Beijing and tending small furry pets seemed absurd, or so it was deemed when we arrived.

So we set off one afternoon to escort Henrietta to a military installation on the outskirts of Beijing. With a couple of million Chinese under arms, I hoped that at least one of them would know something about cats.

Chinese army installations do not appear on tourist maps, so we drove around for a couple of hours before we found an ocher-colored building that housed the Beijing garrison's veterinary station.

The army veterinarian on duty was a lanky, dour soldier with large hands, which he employed to poke and prod Henrietta, thrusting his unwashed fingers into every orifice, oblivious to her screeches of protest. The veterinarian could have been purchasing a new mule for a mountain artillery battery.

But he handled Henrietta deftly before wiping his hands on

his white coat and announcing that, yes, the American cat would be permitted to live with us in Beijing. More important, he stamped a People's Liberation Army veterinary *chop,* or seal, all over her papers, thereby making official Henrietta's new status as a legitimate resident of China.

A week later, we moved Henrietta out of the Beijing Hotel and into our seventh-floor apartment at Jianguomenwai, a new compound built to house Beijing's growing community of foreigners. A young French diplomat lived next door, but his embassy agreed to swap the apartment for one across the compound that was allotted to the new *Times* bureau. By adding the office to our residence, we picked up an extra bedroom for Celia, who otherwise would have had to share a bunk bed with Chris in his small bedroom.

In the course of a little more than four years on three continents, Celia and Chris were moving on to their fifth schools. We had considered putting both our children into a Chinese public school until an Italian journalist and his wife warned us about the downside: their children, they said, were segregated in the rear of the classroom and treated with benign neglect. The Chinese teachers, it seemed, feared getting on the bad side of the Communist Party's ideological watchdogs if they spent too much time helping the foreign children.

As a result, our new friends said, their kids had learned little beyond rudimentary Chinese and had made no fast friends among their Chinese classmates, whose parents feared that contamination by Western kids would hurt their own child's prospects for advancement. The Cultural Revolution, in which hundreds of thousands of educated Chinese had been exiled to menial jobs in the countryside for being contaminated by foreign influences, was still a recent nightmare for many people.

Chris started at the Beijing International School, which was run by a group of English-speaking embassies. But the school ended with the eighth grade, and Celia was starting the ninth grade.

So we sent off her to a recommended boarding school in New Hampshire that I shall coyly refer to as St. Porsche's. There, Celia suffered the re-entry crisis that afflicts many expatriate children who come home after years abroad, only to find their richly textured, even exotic experiences ridiculed as uncool and weird in the trendily insular world of American adolescence.

The other students, Celia reported, were more preoccupied with clothes and parties than with how the rest of the world lived. "Their biggest fear in life is falling off the gravy train," she confided in one letter.

Celia gave a speech about traveling with Henrietta that delighted her teachers and made her a finalist in the school's speech competition. Her affluent classmates at St. Porsche's wondered why anyone would choose a cat for a companion when they could hang out at a shopping mall. Increasingly homesick for us and, yes, for Henrietta, Celia scored straight A's in her first-term exams. Then she left.

Jaqueline returned to help Celia pack, and they caught the next flight to China. Henrietta was thrilled to be reunited with Celia and insisted upon sleeping on her bed every night.

In Beijing, Celia enrolled in the École Française at the French Embassy in Beijing and emerged speaking fluent French. She felt welcome among her new classmates from France, Belgium, Switzerland, and West Africa.

By now Chris had thrown himself into the colorful street life of Beijing. It was a city a twelve-year-old could explore without parental worries. Chris wandered the *hutong*s, or back streets, on his bicycle, practicing the Chinese he was learning at school. But for his blond hair and blue eyes, he hardly stood out among the city's pedaling masses.

As his Chinese improved, Chris hung out at the informal stamp exchange behind the Beijing post office, swapping his American and European stamps to local collectors for rarer Chinese stamps predating the Cultural Revolution.

Yet Celia and Chris never outgrew Henrietta. She would greet their return home from school, when they would sit down with Jaqueline for tea and cookies. Then she would amble over to the *Times* bureau, which offered a telex and other equipment to pounce on. And the nooks and crannies among the piles of books, magazines, and newspapers offered good potential for antimouse surveillance.

During the raw Beijing winter, Henrietta would doze in my office on top of the shortwave radio. Every morning, I used the radio to search out the latest news from the British Broadcasting Corporation and the Voice of America. The rest of the time, the radio reverted to the cat, because its black metal absorbed the warmth of the weak winter sun filtered through a smog of coal fires.

During the Cultural Revolution, between 1966 and 1976, the Maoists lumped cats with intellectuals as societal pests and set about exterminating both of them. By the time we arrived in China, its reform-minded leader, Deng Xiaoping, had rehabilitated the likes of Henrietta with his much-quoted aphorism in defense of pragmatism: "It doesn't matter whether a cat is black or white; if it catches mice, it's a good cat."

The Chinese written character is particularly ingenious about expressing connoting this primal compact between cat and mankind, even in China. The ideogram for *mao,* or cat, incorporates the identifying element, or radical, of an animal, with additional elements denoting a claw, a field, and grass or bamboo, and looks like this:

貓

But the subtext of Chairman Deng's aphorism was that a cat had to pull its weight like everyone else. When Celia was still at St. Porsche's, I wrote her that we had apprenticed Henrietta to Old One-Eyed Chang, an overseer whom I invented for the new construction site adjoining our compound. After initial balking, I wrote, Henrietta was contributing one yuan—about thirteen cents—a day to her upkeep by dragging one brick after another up a rickety wooden ramp. I wondered whether China's now-discredited *tieguofan,* or iron rice bowl, in which every comrade was assured a living wage without having to work hard for it, blunted even mousing skills.

I later wrote an article about the ecological havoc that ensued after the Chinese authorities, having claimed sovereignty over a disputed coral islet in the South China Sea, put ashore some cats to kill the rats that were eating the migratory birds. The cats turned feral and fought one another instead of the rats, prompting the authorities to send in dogs, which did nothing to restore the islet's fragile environment.

In fact, the Chinese seemed far less sentimental than Russians about pets, including cats. In the *chengyu,* or four-character proverbs, that Chinese like to quote, cats are hardly coddled. One *chengyu* says, "The cat leaves when the dog arrives," which seems obvious. And feigning sorrow is dismissed as *mao ku laoshu,* or a cat weeping over a mouse it has killed.

For all the stunning creativity in Chinese art, I cannot recall offhand the celebration of cats found in Japanese art. One Qing Dynasty silk painting I saw showed a cat curled up next to a blooming peony plant, but the cat was asleep and looked rather like a doorstop. Compare this with the Japanese artist Ando Hiroshige's nineteenth-century wood-block print of a cat perched on a windowsill contemplating Mount Fuji, or with Katsushika Hokusai's painting of a cat sitting and smiling mischeviously at a vibrant butterfly. We know as well as the artist what happens next.

Still, the Chinese share with the Japanese the admirable tradition of respecting age that extends to taking care of wise old cats who are long past their prime.

Another *chengyu* advises, "When you lose a cow, you gain a cat." To be candid, I've been grappling with this Chinese proverb without being enlightened about its cosmic significance. It has something to do, I'm told, with the downside of losing too much weight.

Cats were not neglected when it came to China's contribution to world-class kitsch. One of the more interesting artifacts I acquired during my wanderings abroad was a white ceramic plate found in the port city of Tianjin. It didn't date back to the Qing, Ming, or Sung dynasties. I doubt that it was even more than a few months old. But this plate contained a life-sized cat's face constructed of fake fur with large white plastic whiskers and two glass eyes, one blue and the other yellow.

In Bangkok I heard about classic Siamese cats, called *khao manee,* which do have white fur and paired eyes of blue and yellow or green. The Chinese souvenir looked recognizably like a Siamese cat, but with the face dissected to fit snugly on the plate and packaged attractively inside a plastic bubble suitable for hanging in one's living room to impress friends.

It struck me as noteworthy because except for high-rise buildings—and cat-face plates—the Chinese have historically shown themselves incapable of designing and producing anything truly ugly. Hundreds more plates like mine, all of them made in China, covered an entire wall of the souvenir store. The plate cost only a few dollars, and I figured that I could turn a profit reselling it on a trip to one of the oil-rich desert sheikdoms on the Persian Gulf.

Sadly, when I carried this treasure of mass-produced folk art home to Beijing, Henrietta sniffed it over and walked away in disgust, as if to say, "How would you like the world to see your face here?"

I met with even less enthusiasm from Jaqueline, whose notion of leisure is to sit motionless in front of the French Impressionist collection at the Musée d'Orsay in Paris. My cat-face plate offended her taste even more than Henrietta's.

In the end, we reached a compromise under which Jaqueline stored my plate in the garbage and I did not retrieve it.

Chinese policemen patrolling the gates of Jianguomenwai were less meticulous about keeping out the locals than the KGB had been at Sadovo-Samotechnaya, so it was easy to invite some of our Chinese friends to dinner and drive them in without fear of getting hassled. We also provided showers for American and British students living in the cramped Chinese dormitories, which brought Henrietta other admirers.

However, we became careful about letting her out after a

Chinese lawyer who came for dinner warned us to keep an eye on her because some cats were being trapped for their fur. It seemed unlikely until I came across a newspaper article in Shanghai that reported on twenty-nine peasant pelt traders who had been caught with some snares and carcasses of skinned house cats.

Another Chinese friend said that if we let Henrietta visit the nearby Temple of the Sun Park, where Celia and I went jogging, our neighborhood restaurant might be adding another dish to the menu.

I did not take this seriously either until I traveled south to Guangzhou (historically called Canton), where cat was featured on the menus of some restaurants that also displayed live snakes and caged monkeys to whet the diners' appetites.

A friend of mine at the Chinese Foreign Ministry quipped that he and other Chinese were prepared to eat anything with four legs except a table, anything that flew except an airplane, and anything that swam except a submarine.

One popular delicacy couched its contents in the euphemisms of which the Chinese are so fond. A dish eloquently titled "The Dragon Contends with the Tiger and the Phoenix" was basically a thin stew containing equal parts of snake, cat, chicken, and coriander. A restaurant where I dined in Guangzhou one evening served civet cat as an entree, as well as dog and snake.

Civet cats tend to come from Central Africa, or so I am told, where they are prized more for the musk produced by their glands than for their taste as a delicacy. The odds, then, were excellent that the civet cat on the menu was actually a domestic cat who had taken the wrong way home through one of Guangzhou's back alleys.

I tried not to think about all this when, purely in the spirit of good investigative reporting, I ordered the cat. I felt sufficiently bad about it that I never told Henrietta.

It arrived smothered in a thick brown sauce, but the meat looked so stringy that I understood why our ancient ancestors had selected cats over crayfish for domestication. In any case, I couldn't manage more than a taste.

The braised dog tasted better. Peasants I had talked to in northeastern China considered dog a nourishing and therapeutic winter meal. I bought a pair of cowhide boots lined with dog fur in Harbin. No imagination was required to speculate where the rest of the dog had gone.

The tastiest dish in Guangzhou was a snake soup flavored with orange peel and other spices, which I would eat again. Snake tastes a lot like chicken, which I already knew, having eaten a snake in the South Carolina swamps during my army training.

Our first cook in Beijing, a portly man named Mr. Li, was terrified of Henrietta, which I think had a great deal to do with the superstitions passed down among Chinese peasants. Whenever Henrietta tried to enter the kitchen, Cook Li would flap his apron and hiss at our cat.

"Her eyes are shooting sparks at me!" he protested.

Having Henrietta around drove him to quit after a few weeks, contending that working for a foreign family was too strenuous.

His initial complaint baffled me until I discovered that Chinese peasants attributed magic powers to *maoyanshi,* or cat's eyes, and in the old days had used the shape of the cat's pupils to tell what time it was. Feline eyes were slanted at midday, or so the logic went, and grew rounder and brighter as dusk approached.

Li was soon replaced by Mr. Shi, a younger, better cook who did not mind having Henrietta underfoot. He had an easygoing manner and, as he prepared dinner, would slip Henrietta the odd shrimp ball or pork dumpling. Sometimes Mr. Shi would return from the market with fish for our dinner so fresh that they were still flapping, to the delight of our cat, who would jump up on the sink and could not resist poking the water with her paw.

After sturgeon in Moscow and Nile fish in Cairo, Henrietta's palate turned more finicky in Beijing, and she held out for *huangyu,* a plump but bony fish that originated in the Yellow River a few hundred miles away, or so we were told. You won't be amazed to learn that *huangyu* means "yellow fish" in Chinese.

But *huangyu* was rationed as a delicacy for official banquets. So, every week, Jaqueline had to go to a government-owned store in the Sanlitun neighborhood of Beijing, where she engaged in the kind of rote dialogue more typical of my intensive Chinese course at Cambridge. The Chinese interpretation was left to our bureau's enterprising young driver, Mr. Liu, who had previously worked for the French Embassy and spoke not English but French. Jaqueline began by announcing, *"Je voudrais acheter un huangyu,"* and left it to the indispensible Mr. Liu to translate from French to Chinese and back.

"Please, I would like to buy a yellow fish," Jaqueline would say. She couldn't just explain, "I want the yellow fish for my cat," because she would have been turned down.

"Yellow fish are available for official banquets only," the saleslady would reply.

"The yellow fish is required for an official banquet," Jaqueline would say.

"For what official banquet is the yellow fish required?" the saleslady would ask.

"The yellow fish is required for the official banquet hosted by the American newspaper *The New York Times,*" Jaqueline would explain, implying that Deng Xiaoping and the rest of the Chinese politburo were coming around for a fish dinner and a game of mah-jongg.

The saleslady would walk to the back of the shop, out of sight of ordinary customers, fetch a precious *huangyu,* and slap it on the counter for Jaqueline to carry home and debone for the edification of not the diplomatic corps but our cat.

My dear wife returned to the fish counter at Sanlitun and repeated this dialogue every week on Henrietta's behalf. The saleslady never seemed to tire of it, except for those days when she abruptly ended the conversation with a snippy *"Huangyu meiyou."* This freely translated as "No yellow fish today, comrade, tough luck."

I would not be surprised to learn that Jaqueline's regular appearances at the fish counter were duly noted in our dossiers tucked away in the security police files of the Public Security Bureau in Beijing. Henrietta's finicky eating habits may well have earned us the unwarranted reputation as hedonists more obsessed with throwing dinner banquets for diplomats and other foreign devils than with reporting the great achievements of the People's Republic of China.

Sometimes, as I said, the *huangyu* ran out, confronting Henrietta with the reality of socialist economics. Then we had little choice but to feed her table scraps. She preferred Mr. Shi's leftover shrimp and pork dumplings, of course, but turned up her whiskers at anything overseasoned with ginger or coriander.

We tried to monitor what our cat ate, out of concern that Henrietta not succumb to the condition that Western diplomats in Beijing privately referred to as "death by duck."

This alluded to some middle-aged, overweight tourist who would arrive in China out of shape and, without recovering from jet lag, be hustled through the Forbidden City, the Summer Palace, and the Ming tombs, rushed gasping up the stone stairs of the Great Wall, and then, without benefit of a nap, bused off to a sumptuous banquet, the centerpiece of which would be fatty Peking duck. This culinary delicacy is not only utterly mouth-watering but also capable of doubling your cholesterol count at a single sitting. Finally the tourist would be bused back to his hotel and puff up to his room, where his heart would rebel, and, as one of the diplomats euphemistically phrased it, "Whammo! Another death by duck."

We couldn't entirely control what Henrietta chose to eat. Much to our chagrin, she developed a taste for another local creature that inhabited our apartment at Jianguomenwai. Beijing may not lay claim to having the world's biggest cockroaches, but the Chinese variety would be a contender for the most fertile, because they proliferated like, well, cockroaches.

From Hong Kong, we imported "roach motels," small cardboard boxes with several doors leading to the poisoned bait inside. When the time came to hang out a "no vacancy" sign, you were supposed to chuck the box into the garbage, where any survivors could reproduce and crawl back for another try. The more corpulent roaches could not squeeze into the skimpy little cardboard motels, which left them vulnerable to the Cat of a Hundred Exotic Appetites.

"When there are mice around the palace, a crippled cat is

worth more than a fast horse," another Chinese proverb says. The same would apply to cockroaches around the kitchen.

We were washing up after dinner one night when I heard a distinct crunching behind me. I turned around and saw Henrietta, having eaten her fill of yellow fish with carrots and rice, chewing on a savory cockroach for dessert. She swallowed, smacked her lips, and looked up as if to say, "Sure, it's a dirty job, but someone's got to do it. And besides, they're delicious." She spotted another cockroach and could not restrain herself from pouncing, just as you or I would have trouble passing up a bowl of salted nuts.

This left me with what the Chinese call a *maodun,* or contradiction in thought. On one hand, what Henrietta was doing looked disgusting, because who wants to cuddle a cat with roaches on its breath? On the other, she was making real progress with our kitchen's insect population.

I took the pragmatic way out and let feline nature run its course, adapting Chairman Deng's overarching wisdom to the premise that "It doesn't matter whether a cat is Chinese or American; if it gets rid of the cockroaches at no additional expense, it's a good cat."

Henrietta's biggest weakness was herbal tea bags, which, even more than catnip, turned her positively frisky. We had packed into our sea freight some packages of "Good Night Tea" that Jaqueline had bought in Cambridge. Herbal tea was one of those delicacies that we tried to take to each posting as a reminder of life back home, like the maple syrup and Vermont cheddar cheese that traveled in our air luggage.

No sooner did our sea shipment from England arrive than Henrietta chewed right through the cardboard, twine, and wrapping paper of one packing box, extracted the herbal tea bags, and set to chewing them into pulp as we ate dinner.

We found her wriggling with delight on her back, munching an herbal tea bag between her claws, pausing from time to time to race about the apartment for exercise. She also enjoyed Chinese herbal tea, though not with the same fervor. I was reluctant to examine the contents of a Chinese herbal tea bag, having once been served some delicious crispy fried greens in Sichuan that looked suspiciously like marijuana leaves.

Though most of the local cats in Beijing looked like Henrietta, I heard tales of a breed of shaggy wildcat in Sichuan Province, in southwestern China, that looked like the offspring of a romantic tryst between a lynx and a domestic cat. It is said to grow a couple of feet long and is so shy as to be seldom seen.

I had a chance to look into the report when I visited the Wolong Nature Preserve in Sichuan. Wolong is best known as the habitat of the giant panda, which the Chinese call *xiongmao,* literally a bearcat. When I was there, the serenity of the thickly wooded mountains and its waterfalls was interrupted by dynamite blasting to carve out a hydroelectric station at the edge of the nature preserve. Convoys of logging trucks rumbled along the twisting dirt roads. Small wonder that pandas were afraid to descend to eat the arrow bamboo that provided their food staple. If you were an endangered species, would you be sunning yourself anywhere near a logging road? The only pandas I encountered were in captivity at the scientific research station, where one swatted me when I took its picture and tore my jeans with its claws. As for the elusive wildcats, no one at the station reported seeing any, though they were said to range as far afield as Tibet.

In Moscow, we had imported cat litter at some expense from Stockmann's department store in Helsinki, Finland. In Cairo, we had improvised by scooping sand for Henrietta from the surrounding desert.

No such natural resource existed in Beijing, a city more renowned for enough coal dust suspended in the air to gag both man and beast. Jogging in Beijing through the winter months became a form of exercise measurably less healthy for the lungs than chain-smoking two packs of cigarettes a day.

For a while, we tried shredding up the *Renmin Ribao* (*People's Daily*) newspaper. But Henrietta, accustomed to sinking her claws into something more substantial than propaganda before performing her toilette, dismissively scattered the official Communist Party organ all over our bathroom.

Training our cat to settle for shredded newspaper in her litter box did not seem like the greatest idea for someone in my line of work. We had an overabundance of newspapers lying about our apartment as well as in my bureau office because we kept meaning to read them or had marked articles that ought to be clipped and filed away. So many newspapers in tempting piles of disarray presented Henrietta with what the Chinese call a "negative example." I didn't want our cat to conclude that the newspapers were heaped up to accommodate her personal needs.

There is nothing like genuine cat litter, as you will know if you have cats and have read the obituary of one Edward Lowe in *The New York Times* back in October 1995. According to Robert McG. Thomas, a recently deceased colleague who brought a master touch to writing obituaries, Ed Lowe's serendipitous invention of Kitty Litter a half century ago made him into a multimillionaire.

"Cats have been domesticated since ancient Egypt," Bob

Thomas wrote, "but until a fateful January day in 1947, those who kept them indoors full-time paid a heavy price. For all their vaunted obsession with paw-licking cleanliness, cats, whose constitutions were adapted for arid desert climes, make such an efficient use of water that they produce a highly concentrated urine that is one of the most noxious effluences of the animal kingdom."

Sand, sawdust, or wood shavings absorbed some of the pungent smell, Bob continued, "but not enough to make cats particularly welcome in discriminating homes."

So when a neighbor asked Ed Lowe for some of the sawdust that his shop was selling to sop up grease and oil spills, Lowe instead gave her some granulated clay that he carried as a fireproof alternative to sawdust. The neighbor returned for more, and the lucrative cat litter industry was born.

Anyway, on an early trip to Hong Kong, I purchased a twelve-kilo sack of Oko-Pet Hygienic Cat Litter to bring back for Henrietta. This unusual carry-on item caused no lack of curiosity at the security checkpoint in Hong Kong's Kai Tak International Airport, where the inspectors puzzled over the sack, X-rayed it, and instructed me to open it. I must have been smuggling fiendishly disguised narcotics, they surmised, because who would lug around twenty-six pounds, six ounces of cat litter without a cat in sight to show for it?

To compound the confusion, the security personnel spoke Cantonese, a dialect largely unintelligible to native speakers of *putonghua,* the standard (Mandarin) Chinese I had learned at Cambridge.

The two languages use the same Chinese characters but pronounce them quite differently, so in theory I could have vaulted over the linguistic barrier by writing down Henrietta's needs.

But the characters I had memorized at Cambridge had been selected to help me cope with more mundane topics such as diplomatic communiqués, harvest estimates, and *People's Daily* editorials, none of which employed specialized terms for the bodily functions of cats.

The Chinese word for cat—*mao*—is quite a close approximation of our "meow," particularly when it is pronounced correctly in the flat first tone of standard Chinese.

But *mao* is a common homonym that can also mean hair, a feather, grass, a spear, a hat, an anchor, an octogenarian, even a yak, among other more more obscure meanings, not to mention the surname of the late Chairman Mao Zedong. It depends on which of four tones you use in speaking standard Chinese. And the basic *mao* changes in tone if you add the prefix *xiong* for either tomcat or panda. As I was but a few months out of Cambridge, my tones were still shaky.

I finally allayed the concerns of the security staff at Kai Tak Airport by mewing *mao* as plaintively as possible while miming a cat busy with its litter box. Only later did I hear that some Chinese translate a cat's meow as not only *mao* but also *ming,* the all-purpose sound used to imitate animals, birds, and insects.

By now the inspectors' discreet giggles had erupted into outright guffaws, and they merrily waved me onward to my flight to Beijing without making me sift the contents of my carry-on by hand.

Once aboard the Chinese jetliner, my cat litter prompted no concern whatsoever among the other passengers and flight attendants, who were busily cramming electric fans, transistor radios, videocassette recorders, small television sets, and other containers brimming with loot from Hong Kong into the overhead compartments, under the seats, and into the aisles.

Henrietta, of course, was delighted to feel the imported kiln-dried clay flying about under her claws again.

After we settled in to Beijing, Henrietta, with her fondness for exploration, found herself a hideaway high on a bookshelf in the *Times* bureau. While I wrote my articles, her gray head peeked out from behind a half-dozen bound volumes of the collected works of Mao Zedong. It was cool there, and she was undisturbed because I didn't need to consult Chairman Mao anymore about his theory that "All reactionaries are paper tigers." Henrietta already knew that.

Mao Zedong Thought was filled with allusions to the big cats. In one speech in Wuchang years earlier, Chairman Mao had predicted that the relentless advance of proletarian struggle would reduce the "living tigers, iron tigers, real tigers" of imperialism, feudalism, and capitalist-bureaucratism into "paper tigers, dead tigers, bean-curd tigers." By the time we lived in Beijing, the Chinese were paying much more attention to the flourishing capitalist economies of the "little tigers" of Asia, such as South Korea and Singapore.

One day, I sat down to file an analysis of the latest doings of the Chinese Communist Party, the sort of ideological thumbsucker that is eagerly awaited by, well, dozens of readers among the more than one million subscribers to *The New York Times.*

I couldn't work up much enthusiasm for my task and paused to stroke our cat, who had emerged from behind Mao Zedong's collected thoughts to pounce on the keys of my telex machine. Henrietta—so far, I've resisted referring to her as Meow Zedong—relished the privacy of her hiding place behind the red-bound volumes. With reform of China's Marxist command economy racing pell-mell toward free-market greed, Mao Zedong Thought had become superfluous to understanding what was inspiring China's broad masses of workers and peasants these days. The new slogan handed down by Chairman Deng Xiaoping himself was *"Laodong zhifu fuyu guanrong":* "Grow rich through labor; getting rich is glorious."

But I had already reported that, so for want of anything better I found myself writing about what it was like to travel around the world with a cat. Henrietta seemed a lot livelier than Mao Zedong Thought, which she found quite literally a snooze, even if it did launch the Cultural Revolution and thereby erase a decade of productivity and well-being from the lives of nearly a quarter of the world's population.

I wrote about Henrietta's adventures during her first decade overseas in Moscow, Cairo, and Beijing and filed the article to the *Times* with the request that my editors on the foreign desk find somewhere to run it. In those days, a chatty piece about the family cat did not yet fit my employers' definition of All the News That's Fit to Print. But they did publish it, prominently, in the Living Section.

Henrietta's life overseas triggered more mail to me from *Times* readers than the most momentous political events I have covered in eighteen years as a foreign correspondent, including Anwar el-Sadat's visit to Israel and Nelson Mandela's release from prison in South Africa.

The interest in Henrietta hardly flagged. It got so that some American tourists visiting China would telephone the *Times* bureau to explain, "We just got in last night and are heading off to see the Great Wall of China, and we want to view your cat on the way back from the Ming tombs before we tour the Forbidden City. Will just before four o'clock be convenient for her? We can't do it tomorrow because we'll be in Xian, or whatever that place is called with all the terra-cotta statues."

I would promise to check Henrietta's appointments schedule.

One day, I received a telephone call from a pleasant woman in Omaha, Nebraska, which was at least thirteen time zones behind China.

"I read the article about your cat and I'm coming to China next week," she began, "and want to—"

I silently groaned.

"—bring something for Henrietta," she continued. "Please tell me what she needs."

I ran next door to our apartment for a quick inventory of our larder, which was running bare of imported foodstuffs.

"Maybe a box or so of American cat food," I replied eagerly. "Henrietta would love just about anything."

A week or two later, the tourist showed up at our front door on the seventh floor at Jianguomenwai. She staggered under a load of so many boxes of Tender Vittles and other feline delicacies as to assure Henrietta a time-share in pussycat Paradise for the foreseeable future. Now Jaqueline could stop making her weekly trips to the fish counter on the pretense of throwing extravagant dinner parties.

Henrietta's visitor refused to be compensated for the cat food, which must have consumed her entire weight allowance on the long flight to Beijing. She was content to sit and deftly scratch the ears of Henrietta, who downed a bowl of goodies before making her way to the benefactor's lap.

During our conversation, I mentioned that Henrietta had lived for four years in Moscow before coming to Beijing, so our cat knew more about life under communism than most Americans. I added that I wanted to write a book someday comparing the two countries. (It was eventually published.) The visitor continued petting Henrietta, who was purring overtime, and dispensed some advice to which I paid scant attention at the moment.

"Forget Russia, forget China," she said. "Write about your cat."

Ottawa and New York

As we approached the end of our third year in Beijing, the *Times* asked if I would consider extending our posting for a fourth year. By now my Chinese was proficient enough to allow me to read wall posters and interview people on the street. There were only two provinces out of China's twenty-nine provinces and autonomous regions that I not visited.

The *Times* seemed gratified when I agreed, and the matter was settled.

A few months thereafter, I got a call from Warren Hoge, the new foreign editor, one of whose first official duties was to telephone and inquire, "You're a skier, aren't you?"

I looked at the clock. It must have been nearly noon in New York, because it was nearly midnight in Beijing.

"Yes," I told Warren, "I do like to ski."

"Chris," Warren said, "you're going to love the new assignment."

Now, Warren is one of the most gracious and considerate people you'll meet at the *Times,* so I knew he hadn't called me that late to discuss snow conditions in Manchuria.

"What new assignment?" I asked suspiciously.

"Being our new bureau chief in Ottawa," Warren said.

Never let it be said that *The New York Times* doesn't try to keep its far-flung correspondents well informed.

"By the way, how's the cat?" he asked.

All right, maybe Warren asked about the family rather than Henrietta. The time had come for another musical-chairs reshuffle of reporters around the world. We didn't talk long because he had to call John Burns in Moscow, who was going to replace me, so I would replace Mike Kaufman in Ottawa, who was going to Warsaw to dislodge John Darnton, who was returning to New York as deputy foreign editor, sending Barbara Crossette off to Bangkok, and so on.

Still, how could I complain—though I did—when I had been entrusted with three of the *Times's* most demanding line bureaus, with an abundance of great stories, and now was being given a fourth assignment that offered something no less enticing, which was great skiing?

Back-to-back hardship postings in Moscow, Cairo, and Beijing had not been easy on our family, and the prospect of life back in North America had its appeal, not least for our cat. After more than a decade abroad, it was time for Henrietta to rediscover her roots.

We had recently bought a dairy farmer's house on a wooded hill in rural Vermont, only two hours' drive south of Quebec, in part so that Celia and Chris would have someplace to call home. They felt awkward about having to explain to other American kids that, no, they weren't Russian or Egyptian or Chinese, just because they had lived there.

Henrietta fell head over tail in love with Vermont, as I shall explain a little later. A case could be made for putting her portrait on Ben & Jerry's ice-cream containers instead of all those cows.

When I returned to China to finish up my assignment after my next home leave with the family, we spared the cat the seventeen-hour flight back to Beijing and by leaving her with the young schoolteacher who had rented our Vermont house for the winter. Celia and Chris were now studying together

ONTARIO
JZ1 499
YOURS TO DISCOVER

at Northfield Mount Hermon School in Massachusetts, and were not far away from Henrietta.

Our cat extended her vacation into a New England autumn of glorious colors, hunting field mice and exploring the woods and meadows near our house, while Jaqueline and I poked around China's northwestern provinces of Gansu and Ningxia and Inner Mongolia before returning to Beijing to pack. Our departure from China kept getting postponed, and it was not until December that we picked up Henrietta and brought her to Canada.

Let me declare here that I am one of those Americans who count among my nation's blessings its extraordinarily good fortune to have ended up with Canada as our next-door neighbor.

Still, a cordial welcome does not spring to mind when describing our arrival in Ottawa, the Canadian capital where we spent nearly two years. The first Ottawans we met, upon learning that we were American, embarked on a long-winded tale of how their forefathers had chosen to remain loyal to the British Crown by relocating north to Canada rather than hang out with the rabble fighting the American Revolution. I was tempted to propose another theory: that their forefathers had had little choice but to flee after my forefathers had tried to tar and feather them.

For whatever reason, some of our neighbors in Ottawa lived in fear of waking up some morning to discover that they had been annexed by Watertown, New York. I never encountered this prissy nationalism elsewhere in Ontario, nor in Quebec or British Columbia or Newfoundland, where the natives acted pleased, or at least amused, to meet a visiting Yank.

None of this nationalism nonsense fazed Henrietta. I think she knew instinctively that the first cats in North America had been brought to Canada by French Jesuit missionaries in the seventeenth century and that she must be their descendant.

Henrietta would have passed for one of her Canadian cousins but for her giveaway penchant for jaywalking when our stoplight on Crichton Street turned red. Such contempt for the law might not have been condoned in a Canadian cat unless it lived in Quebec, where flouting legislation passed in Ottawa was a popular pastime.

But Ottawa was a tidy city, and Henrietta welcomed its normalcy no less than the rest of us did. I put her to work writing our annual Christmas newsletter to friends and family, with, of course, my hands-on editorial guidance.

"Given the procrastination that runs rampant in this family," her letter explained, "it was left to me to lend a paw."

You might ask how a cat could write a family newsletter, to which I would reply, "Extremely slowly." As a young reporter, I recall being told that animals in news articles would be allowed to speak only with the permission of the managing editor. So I see no reason why a cat shouldn't be permitted to write letters, with the permission of its owner.

In her letter, Henrietta boasted that "I may submit my curriculum vitae to the Guinness Book of World Records as the most travelled cat in the world, with no fewer than four continents in my thirteen years."

She added, "I am getting used to being just another neighborhood cat, and it is nice to wander around incognito without having someone wonder how you would taste in a sweet and sour sauce or asking for your pawprint."

The Canadian authorities acted less concerned with what Henrietta was doing on Canadian soil than with why the rest of us were taking up space. Whenever I entered Canada, the immigration or customs official on duty was guaranteed, I recall, to engage me in a jolly banter that went much like this:

INSPECTOR: Where do you live?
ME: Ottawa.
INSPECTOR: And where were you born in Canada?
ME: Hollywood, California.
INSPECTOR: So you're not Canadian?
ME: I think not.
INSPECTOR: You're an alien residing in Canada, eh?
ME: My wife suspects as much.
INSPECTOR: What are you doing in Canada?
ME: I'm covering it for *The New York Times.*
INSPECTOR: Why can't your job be filled by a Canadian?
ME: You mean, like Peter Jennings's job in New York could be filled by an American? We try to leave those decisions to our respective employers.
INSPECTOR: Eh?
ME: Because Peter Jennings sends a lot more dollars back to Canada than I take out.

For those of you who only read books, Peter Jennings, the evening news anchorman for ABC-TV, was born in Ottawa.

In all candor, my dialogues with the Canadian authorities entailed far more groveling on my part than snappy repartee. I would never claim to have been singled out for harrassment.

After Jaqueline took a volunteer job teaching English to immigrants newly arrived in Ottawa, a local official complained that she was depriving a Canadian of the opportunity to volunteer. Jaqueline was earning not a penny from her labors, which I suspect was why no hoard of unemployed Canadians was vying to replace her.

But whenever we drove Henrietta back and forth across the border between Canada and Vermont, the Canadian authorities never bothered to inquire, "Has your furry American companion been catching mice that a Canadian cat should be harvesting?"

I took this as evidence that Canada has nothing against cats, giving us Americans one more good reason to prize it as a neighbor, however pettily a few of its bureaucrats may behave. Canadians, after all, have had similar run-ins with the eight-hundred-pound gorilla across their border.

During one trip to Toronto, I interviewed the Royal Canadian Air Farce, a comedy troupe responsible for the most hilarious political satire in North America. When I introduced myself as the *Times* correspondent in Ottawa, they feigned sympathy: Had I realized that Ottawa is the only major city in Canada whose name begins with zero?

Don Ferguson, one of the troupe members, put me at ease by volunteering that he loved to visit our country. "The thrill about going to the United States," he deadpanned, "is that you know everybody's armed."

Curiously, Henrietta could tell the difference between Ontario and Vermont. No sooner would we cross the Canadian border to Vermont than our cat would awake from her nap and start dancing with delight. She would stand on her hind legs with front paws balanced on the window glass, whiskers twitching, and then race to the other side of the car and look out again.

By the time we headed up the steep dirt road to our Vermont house, Henrietta could scarcely contain her excitement. I don't know how she knew we had returned to the closest place we called home in the United States. There must have been something Proustian in the fragrance of fir and spruce trees and freshly mown meadows that evoked for Henrietta the harvesting of field mice past.

How effortlessly did our cat—who had ridden on sleek jetliners to visit some of the great cities of the world, grown attuned to the babble of strange languages, and held audiences for admiring tourists in countless airport lounges—revert to her primordial instinct as the natural huntress. I never failed to be struck by Henrietta's quick familiarity with the outdoors, though the fascination was hardly new.

A century and a half earlier, the writer Henry David Thoreau observed a cat that had ventured into the remote woods around his solitary hut on Walden Pond in Massachusetts.

"Once I was surprised to see a cat walking along the stony shore of the pond, for they rarely wander so far from home," Thoreau wrote in *Walden*. "The most domestic cat, which has lain on a rug all her days, appears quite at home in the woods and, by her sly and stealthy behavior, proves herself more native there than the regular inhabitants."

I don't want you to conclude that Henrietta just goofed off in Vermont, because her days were packed with more activities than a cruise director could hope to devise. A typical day unfolded much like this:

5:30 A.M.	Wake up the family, demanding to be let out.
5:45 A.M.	Wake us up again, demanding to be let in.
6:10 A.M.	Demand to go out again.
6:20 A.M.	Demand to be let in for breakfast.
6:30 A.M.	Postprandial toilette, licking, etc.
6:45 A.M.	Depart on patrol to inspect how our eighteen acres of woodland had fared overnight.
8:00 A.M.	Return with comatose field mouse.

8:15 A.M. Finish concealment of mouse under our bed, within bathtub, behind door, etc.

8:20 A.M. Revisit breakfast.

8:30 A.M. Embark upon long-range reconnaissance of our neighbors' meadows and forests.

10:00 A.M. Return bearing trophy chipmunk.

10:05 A.M. Formal presentation of trophy chipmunk to Jaqueline.

10:15 A.M. Meditation period under bird feeder, gazing up at visiting birds in posture of eschatological expectation.

10:30 A.M. Back inside for drink of water.

10:45 A.M. Inspection of basement and heating ducts for fresh rodent spoor, etc.

I'm sure you get the idea, because by midafternoon, Henrietta was exhausted enough to prostrate herself in the shade of one of our sugar maple trees, resting up for her sunset prowl.

Once when we drove from Vermont to Illinois for the wedding of my niece Sharon Moore, we were hesitant to park Henrietta in a local cat-care facility. So Henrietta went to Sharon's wedding, driving through Canada and back with nary a peep from Canadian border officials. Of course, this may have been because she was dozing under a blanket.

Henrietta's only real adventure on that journey consisted of sharing our hotel with the Chicago Bears during their summer training. To avoid being stepped on by extremely large, rambunctious young men carrying footballs during her exploration of the hotel corridors, Henrietta employed the dexterity she had developed in Egypt to avoid being trampled by camels.

Henrietta had seen plenty of snow in Russia, but she soon learned that it didn't compare with what overflowed our backyard in Canada.

Our cat would plead to be let out through the back door, upon which she would drop to the frozen ground and disappear inside the snowdrifts, which sometimes reached thigh-deep (my thigh, not Henrietta's) after a good storm.

By the time Jaqueline started fretting about what had become of Henrietta, she was reassured by frenetic mewing, but this time from the front door.

As soon as Jaqueline opened it, the cat, her fur matted with melting snow and ice dripping from her paws, trotted in to find a place by the kitchen stove, with nary a thank-you. You would think she had learned her lesson, but within minutes she ventured out again, teaching herself to plow through the drifts with the verve of a snow leopard, or at least a sled dog.

Unlike some other cats I've seen, Henrietta was not content to spend the day inside drowsing by the hearth. Her embrace of winter seemed more natural to me after Will Steger, a Minnesota explorer leading a dogsled expedition to the North Pole, invited me along one February on a training run across the pack ice off Baffin Island, which weatherwise lies on the blustery windward side of Greenland.

Making small dogs pull large sleds seemed like an act of cruelty. But there was something so romantic for readers of newspapers about a jet-age attempt to take an old-fashioned sled to the North Pole that I dug out my warmest down parka and boots and flew from Montreal to Iqaluit, as the largest town in Canada's eastern Arctic is called. On my first night, the local radio station cheerily reported that the temperature had dipped modestly, to a brisk 54 degrees below zero Fahrenheit.

Such bracing weather did not deter Will and his five teammates, who expected that it would turn really cold once they headed north. When I joined them, Will was busy harnessing his dogs. Ear-splitting shrieks arose from kennels. It sounded as if a dog were being flayed alive until Will explained that his lead dog, Critter, was expressing outrage at not being taken along because of an injured paw.

"The worst punishment you could do to our dogs is to leave them behind," Will said. "They live to pull."

I accepted this with a reporter's ingrained skepticism, mentally daring the rest of the dogs to prove me wrong. They bounded off like hounds in pursuit of a rabbit while I clung on to the sled to avoid getting flung overboard. These dogs were clearly doing what they loved. Whenever we wanted to stop, we had to cast out a kind of anchor that snagged on a passing chunk of ice, jolting sled and dogs to an involuntary standstill. So much for my assumptions of cruelty. There was nary a whip in sight.

The only menacing item was the large high-powered hunting rifle that Will eased into a padded case and strapped onto the middle sled.

"Polar bears," Will said laconically.

Polar bears, I learned later, are as nearsighted as I am and interpret anything moving on the icy horizon as dinner, which on this trip would have included the sled dogs and me. I had no illusion about who among us was expendable. The expedition could afford to lose a newspaper reporter to a ravenous polar bear and still reach the top of the world before the spring thaw. But running out of dogs on the journey would portend failure and even disaster after the last newspaperman was eaten.

I felt relief that I hadn't given in to my first thought of taking Henrietta with me to the Arctic. And I made sure to stay close to the sled carrying the gun.

I spent a surprisingly cozy night in an igloo that Will and his comrades kindly hacked out to keep me from freezing to death. The dogs slept outside, content to curl up in the snow despite the subzero Arctic temperatures, digesting their frozen slabs of yummy caribou meat and dreaming of jollier times ahead pulling the sled over the ragged pack ice.

After a hearty breakfast consisting mostly of butter—Will and his teammates consumed seven thousand greasy calories a day and came home with cholesterol levels too low for medical researchers at the University of Minnesota to chart—I bade the gang farewell and putt-putted back over the ice to Baffin Island in the deafening comfort of a local Inuit's snowmobile.

Will Steger and his expedition did reach the North Pole without me, proving to the world, among other achievements, a basic difference between dogs and cats. Had they harnessed a team of cats like Henrietta to their sleds, I can confidently predict that they would still be in transit. Oh, the cats might have tugged a little this way and that. Then they would have sat down as if to say, "Okay, guys, your turn to haul us."

And while sled dogs were perfectly content to cuddle in a snowdrift for the night, sled cats would have insisted upon a place inside the igloo and demanded to be let out and in, out and in.

Everybody knows that the Inuit, or Eskimos, employ a variety of different words for snow, depending on its consistency and condition, just as we rattle off the brand names of fast-food franchises whose products taste pretty much the same. But when I traveled in Canada's western Arctic to Tuktoyaktuk, on the frozen shores of the Beaufort Sea, the local Eskimo dialect, Inuvialuktun, employed at least three separate words to describe generically the sort of animals likely to be encountered when one was out and about:

Pamiqsaaq meant "a domesticated animal"—Henrietta the cat, for example.

Nuyittuq meant "a wild animal unafraid of man," perhaps a caribou.

And *nuyuaqtuyuq* was a totally wild animal, such as a polar bear, though it would not seem far-fetched to describe a cranky polar bear as *nuyittuq* if it was hungrily rummaging through the garbage cans outside your igloo and your distraught spouse expected you to get out of bed and shoo it away.

There was another useful word that I copied down for Henrietta, knowing that she would never pronounce it correctly. My source in the western Arctic, a philologist who was beavering away on a dictionary in Inuvialuktun, passed it on as the longest word he had transcribed so far, and it seemed right up Henrietta's alley: *Tuktusiuriagatigitqingnapin'ngitkiptin'nga,* which might best be translated as "You'll never go hunting caribou with me again."

Having survived the winter snows, Henrietta gave us another scare when the basement of our rented house flooded during Ottawa's spring thaw. The basement was not a finished one, which allowed Henrietta to probe its nooks and crannies, much like a spelunker in a cave.

One night, the basement filled with so much water that some of our storage boxes were left floating. Jaqueline had seen Henrietta venture down there, but when she looked, the cat was nowhere to be seen. Jaqueline visualized Henrietta clinging to some floating board for survival. At last Jaqueline waded back upstairs to our kitchen, having concluded that our cat had drowned in the basement's icy currents.

Gently, Jaqueline prepared us for the worst. Henrietta, she said, had lived a fuller life than anyone could have expected of a thirteen-year-old cat. She was winding up her touching eulogy when Henrietta trotted up out of the waterlogged basement, looking dry as a bone, and set to work cleaning the rest of the food from her bowl.

We grew more worried about a curious habit that our cat developed in Ottawa. Henrietta took to licking or chewing at her fur, usually concentrating on one spot, and then biting at the skin exposed by her rough tongue. The veterinarians whom we consulted supposed that such fur biting was a neurotic habit. The puzzle was why Henrietta was doing it in Canada when she had never chewed her fur overseas, even while she was recovering from the trauma of living wild in Cairo's backstreets.

We took her to see a veterinary specialist who proposed solving the problem by fitting a stiff Elizabethan-type collar over Henrietta's neck to prevent the cat from licking her fur. Jaqueline considered this advice, which had not been inexpensive, then asked the specialist, "How would you like to go around wearing an Elizabethan collar?"

The next veterinarian was more sympathetic to Henrietta's plight. He prescribed prednisone, a mild steroid that did discourage her from excessive licking but caused her to race around a bit.

Jaqueline later came up with a diagnosis of her own: Henrietta, she pointed out, had begun chewing at her fur only after returning to North America and switching full-time to canned cat food. Her organic diet in Cairo and Beijing, Jaqueline suggested, must have rendered her allergic to the preservatives with which supermarket pet food is laced.

Contrary to my initial trepidation, our cat had thrived overseas on fish cooked with rice and vegetables topped off with a savory mouse or cockroach for dessert. Plus, of course, the occasional dollop of nutritious caviar, which I recommend as a stimulant for any cat's appetite, if you can afford it. Henrietta had not been indulged with caviar since I had been expelled from Iran and returned to Cairo bearing a woven silk carpet for my spouse and for everyone else, including Henrietta, a two-pound can of quality fish eggs scooped from a Beluga sturgeon netted in the Caspian Sea. One of the things I like about Iran is that when its government throws you out, you get enough time to spend some dollars on caviar for your cat at the duty-free shop before you're put aboard the next flight out of Tehran International Airport.

In any case, Jacqueline was right, and Henrietta stopped biting her fur when we later moved back overseas and returned to preparing her food from raw ingredients.

Cats are celebrated finicky eaters, more so than dogs, but Henrietta was given so little choice overseas that she did not snub her food bowl. I once read a study from Paris that reported that half of the cats and dogs in France were overweight. But what surprised me about the study was that 10 percent of the French cats and 4 percent of the dogs were obese to the point that their health was threatened. So you may imagine what the obesity rate must be like for pampered American pets.

Yet as long as Henrietta traveled with us, she never had a weight problem. So by having to improvise Henrietta's food from the basic ingredients on hand in Russia, Egypt, and China, we may have done her a favor.

Our tour in Canada included some temporary assignments for me, first in the Philippines and then in Tunisia and Egypt, before I was summoned back to New York to become an assistant foreign editor. I had mixed emotions about giving up reporting to become an editor, though I wanted to learn about another side of the *Times* and the money was better.

It became our first assignment that Henrietta could drive to, from Ottawa to New York City via the New York State Thruway. By contrast, when Beirut collapsed into anarchy, my colleague John Kifner had to evacuate his cats by hiding their cage under the departing load of a television network's gear bound for Cyprus.

Henrietta was not happy to find herself confined to the kind of Manhattan apartment that a real estate agent might describe as a "cozy 2BR w/airshaft vu." The *Times* put us up there until we could find our own place, but there wasn't much for Henrietta to explore for more than thirty seconds.

After a mere five months of incessant searching, we succeeded in finding, buying, painting, and rewiring a roomier cooperative apartment that we could barely afford on Manhattan's Upper West Side, a half-dozen blocks north of where we had lived when Henrietta had originally acquired us.

For me, becoming an editor at the *Times* was an eye-opener, for I had never fully grasped the complex dialectic between editor and reporter.

No longer were the editors (of whom I was now one) tone-deaf, insensitive louts who set ludicrously early deadlines for us hardworking, death-defying, plucky lads and lasses in the field so they, the editors would have more time to lick the last sandwich mayonnaise from their fingers before whacking away at our exquisitely crafted little jewel-box stories with a proverbial mallet and cleaver.

It now dawned upon me that we editors had been grievously underappreciated by foreign correspondents, those sniveling, self-indulgent perpetual adolescents (of whom I had been a prime example) who wrote too long and filed too late, requiring editors to save the day by pruning and polishing their hastily written stories on deadline, with a proverbial mallet and cleaver if necessary.

I knew about the hardships of working abroad and harbored a nostalgia for heat and dust. While running the foreign desk on weekends, I once talked long-distance with a friend in a country where I had worked and realized that I had traded adventure for a telephone with twelve buttons.

Doubtless Henrietta missed it too. Becoming just another cat in a New York City apartment was a letdown. She too had traded adventure for a sofa by a high-rise window that caught the morning sun.

So when the *Times* bureau in South Africa opened up, I asked for it. Joe Lelyveld, who had become foreign editor (and eventually became the newspaper's executive editor), was sympathetic, having served two tours as the *Times* correspondent in South Africa. The Johannesburg bureau was mine if I wanted it, he said. Then he went to the heart of the problem.

"Does Jaqueline want to go back overseas?" he asked.

I confessed that I thought not but would ask her. We were settled comfortably in New York City. Jaqueline enjoyed her job as a school librarian and liked walking home through Central Park. Celia was at Harvard, and Chris would soon graduate from Northfield Mount Hermon School, so neither of them was that far away.

I raised the prospect cautiously that same evening, after complimenting Jaqueline on the superb cheeseburgers and frozen spinach that she prepared for our dinner and telling her, by the way, that she had never looked slimmer. I had braced myself for an adamant refusal until I saw a telltale twinkle in her hazel eyes.

"Why don't we ask the children what they think?" she proposed.

"Let's tell them how thrilled Henrietta would be," I pressed on helpfully. "She looks so terribly bored here."

I turned to our cat and, without trying to influence her in the least, asked, "Henrietta, wouldn't you really rather go back overseas? To South Africa? Meet some lion cousins? And chase a few giraffes?"

Henrietta, who had never seen a giraffe, didn't agree to this immediately. No, she stretched for a long time while she mulled over the prospect. After ten or fifteen minutes, she ambled to the window, hopped up on the sill, and looked longingly down on the world outside.

Well, that is about as unequivocal an affirmation as you're likely to tease out of most cats. By the next morning, when she hopped onto Jaqueline's pillow, every sinew rippling under Henrietta's fur fairly screamed, "Yes, by all means, I want to go to South Africa!"

We called Celia and Chris, who cheered and proposed putting aside their studies for a year to join us.

With that unanimous vote, five to zero, I took leave of my fellow game wardens in the *Times* newsroom and defected back to the poachers.

Johannesburg

We flew overnight from New York to Lisbon, filling four seats abreast in the front row of TAP's Navigator Class, which offered Henrietta the occasional view of the glowing controls in the cockpit. She wasn't exactly invited into the cockpit, but the captain did come out to greet *a gata,* which is Portuguese for a feline of the female persuasion.

The flight attendants fussed appropriately over her, giving her tidbits of Portuguese cod and shrimp from the galley. There is nothing to set the heart beating like a comely dark-eyed stewardess who confesses to feeling passionate about your cat.

Our luggage had been checked through to Johannesburg on our connecting flight the following night, so Henrietta had plenty of room to stand on her hind paws and look out the window at Lisbon during our taxi ride. We had rented two rooms at a downtown hotel, but hadn't informed the hotel management that our party included a *gata* in transit among three continents.

Rather than burden them with details, Jaqueline quietly carried the cat—well, maybe smuggled her—to our adjoining rooms while I checked us in. I've learned as a reporter that while you must never misrepresent what you're doing, there's no need to shout it from the rooftops either. And Henrietta was usually pretty good about keeping her whiskers buttoned while we were traveling.

In the bathroom, Celia and Chris poured out a little dry

food for Henrietta, filled her other bowl with water, and spilled some litter into the plastic travel box.

"Don't you think Henrietta would enjoy some milk?" my dear wife asked solicitously.

I couldn't see how. "That gorgeous stewardess kept stuffing her with cod and shrimp and things all through the flight," I said. "How can she have room left for milk—"

"What gorgeous stewardess?" Jaqueline interrupted.

There are too many attractive women in this world not to look. But being happily married to one of them, I can afford to stare with taste instead of appetite.

Before I could explain this nuance about the platonic appeal of the opposite sex, Jaqueline turned to Henrietta and said, "Daddy's calling room service to get you a bowl of cold milk from a Portuguese cow."

Our *gata* looked up expectantly. So I called room service.

"I'd like to order a bowl of milk," I began. "I mean, make that a glass of milk."

"The milk, yes," the voice on the phone politely prompted. "And what else, please?"

"One glass of milk will do us fine," I said.

The Portuguese are nothing if not hospitable. "And something to eat?" the polite voice persisted.

"Not right now," I said, "but we do need our milk."

"Then how many glasses of milk will you need?" he asked.

"Just one glass," I told him. "We're sharing."

Within minutes, a man in a black tuxedo arrived at our door, pushing a cart covered with a dazzling white cloth and a single glass of milk accompanied by a red rose. He looked a bit puzzled about the kind of guests who would come to Lisbon to order a glass of milk when his homeland made such delicious wines.

I did not let him inquire further but reached through the door for the milk, passed it to Jaqueline, signed the bill, added a generous tip to seal his silence, and thanked him profusely.

Greedily, Henrietta slurped up the milk—nothing low-fat here, as Jaqueline had promised.

A couple of mornings later, we arrived in Johannesburg from Lisbon. By the time we crossed the equator, Henrietta's enthusiasm for air travel was stretched thin. From the window, she watched the broad brown expanse of high plains, or veldt, and desert unfold as the TAP jetliner descended. She was impatient to explore Africa in the boldest traditions of Livingstone and Stanley.

As we approached Jan Smuts International Airport, our first impression from the air was that our new posting consisted mostly of swimming pools. Hundreds of them sparkled like turquoise baubles dropped across a verdant carpet of backyards. We had arrived if not in the heart of Africa, then at least somewhere below its waist, yet the view that swept past the airliner's wings evoked the suburban sprawl of Los Angeles. Johannesburg, it turned out, had much in common with the California that I remembered from childhood. The sunshine was abundant, the weather balmy, and air-conditioned shopping malls lined the shady streets. And the distinction between white and black neighborhoods was obvious.

Our landing had taken us over the privileged northern suburbs, where the affluent white minority lived. Only later did we find a more authentic Africa in the dusty townships and squatter camps that blended into the veldt on Johannesburg's southern flank. The disparity was a stark visual introduction to apartheid, which had barred Africans from moving into the better areas reserved for whites, except as domestic servants or day laborers. One could geographically chart the country's rainfall, or more precisely the dearth of it, by the leftover areas assigned to blacks. While formal segregation unraveled during our four years in South Africa, the inequity lingered on the ground.

The veterinarian on duty at Johannesburg's international airport had not shown up, and no one seemed to expect him. We were sleepless from the night flight, and Henrietta was restless. So, after waiting around awhile, we placed the cat's box on an airport cart, piled our suitcases on top, and rolled her through the rest of the immigration and customs formalities. I hesitate to describe Henrietta as having been smuggled. After all, she had just been freshly vaccinated and her papers were in order. We had intended to complete the cat's formalities once everyone had gotten some rest, but it became one of those nagging tasks that we never got around to and later forgot.

After living with the ice and snow of Russia and Canada and the raw, windy cold of China, Henrietta was ready to bask in the African sunshine. No sooner had we arrived in the house we had rented in a suburb of Johannesburg than she tiptoed out to our new garden. She sniffed the grass, poked her whiskers into the ferns and shrubs, and finally curled up in the shade of a leafy tree and fell asleep.

Our carelessness with Henrietta's formalities created a subsequent nightmare after we took her to the United States the next summer for a vacation in Vermont. Jaqueline followed me back to Johannesburg several weeks later, flying with the cat from New York via Frankfurt and Windhoek, Namibia.

When the flight stopped over briefly in Windhoek to let off passengers, Henrietta, despite her vociferous protests, was downgraded from the cabin to the hold for the final two hours of her long intercontinental journey. The Lufthansa representative in Windhoek explained that Henrietta could be deported back to Namibia if South African health officials inspecting the jetliner on arrival in Johannesburg objected to finding her inside the cabin. It was a problem we hadn't encountered flying with the Portuguese, but Germans are nothing if not thorough about bureaucratic details.

Jaqueline related the setback in Henrietta's flight status when I met her on Friday afternoon at Johannesburg's international airport. Together we headed for the baggage claim area, where Jaqueline's suitcases soon appeared—but without Henrietta.

I checked with Lufthansa's baggage representative, who supposed that a cat traveling in the hold would have been diverted to the South African Airways freight terminal. We drove to the freight terminal, which had lots of freight but no sign of Henrietta.

The baggage master, a heavy Afrikaner with a red face, responded to our concern with a surly indifference that tenured employees of the New York Department of Motor Vehicles would envy. No, he said, *die kat* had not been in the freight shipment just arrived from Frankfurt.

Afrikaners tended to be suspicious of foreigners anyway, and especially Americans. They blamed us for undermining the foundations of a racist system that guaranteed semiliterate, incompetent, and otherwise unemployable Afrikaans-speaking whites cushy sinecures in parastatal enterprises from South African Airways to the post office.

The baggage master did not want to waste his time on Henrietta's whereabouts when life offered so many forms to fill out and so little time. He did not object when Jaqueline and I walked into the restricted shed to comb through the incoming airfreight ourselves. Finding a small gray cat amid the avalanche of containers seemed hopeless. It occurred to me that Lufthansa might have left Henrietta sitting on the runway in Windhoek.

We were about to go back to the main terminal and demand the kind of help that Lufthansa and South African Airways should have extended the first time around when Jaqueline gripped my arm. "Can you hear her?" she said.

I listened. A faint but unmistakable mewing drifted up from the jumble of crates, boxes, and bags.

Like rescuers digging for earthquake victims, we pulled away the debris as we honed in on the cat's cage, which at least was right side up.

Henrietta's nose was pressed against the door's metal mesh, frantically sucking in air.

We carried her box over to the baggage master's office, and I produced a matching copy of her waybill. After sorting through the sheaf of papers I handed him, the Afrikaner declared that he could not release our cat because we had no form authorizing her admittance to South Africa. The veterinarian on duty had left for the weekend. We must wait three days to have Henrietta cleared.

"Come back Monday," the baggage master said.

Jaqueline produced something from the cat's veterinarian in Johannesburg showing that she had been living in South Africa and other papers attesting that she had just been vaccinated by Dr. David Webster, our capable veterinarian in Vermont.

The baggage master was unmoved. "Come back Monday," he repeated.

"The cat has no food or water," I protested. "She can't survive without food and water till Monday."

The baggage tender mopped the sweat from his jowls. The terminal was sweltering in the African heat, proving my point.

"I have no authority," he said. "You must come back now."

One of the eccentricities of South African English is that "now" does not necessarily mean "now." More often it means whenever both parties get around to it. If you want something done faster, you say, "just now." Or if you're feeling pushy, you specify that you want it "now-now."

"Now-now?" I pleaded.

He shrugged. "Now." That meant Monday.

I wondered whom I could call at the Foreign Ministry, or even the Presidency, to extract my cat from this South African bureaucratic maw. But I had not brought any telephone numbers with me, and by the time I could locate the helpful Afrikaners who worked there, the baggage master would have locked up Henrietta's waybill with the other unclaimed freight and gone home himself. And no waybill meant no cat until the office reopened.

"Now-now," I insisted.

Henrietta wailed even more piteously, desperate to be freed from her cruel incarceration now that Jaqueline and I had found her. Walking away would break her heart.

After what seemed like an hour of begging, the baggage master wavered, then grudgingly relented. I doubt that my appeal to his conscience or Henrietta's welfare changed his mind. He wanted us out of his shed and knew that Jaqueline or I might well throw ourselves in front of his car to prevent his now-now departure.

We promised to bring Henrietta back on Monday to see the airport veterinarian if only she could leave with us now. Within minutes, Henrietta was out of her box and stretched across Jaqueline's lap in the Johannesburg bureau's BMW, while the air conditioner on full blast ruffled her fur. Within the hour, she had been watered and fed and was reacquainting herself with the shadier parts of our garden.

Jaqueline drove Henrietta back to the airport the following week and cleared up her status. It is tempting to blame the obstinancy that we encountered on the capriciousness of an apartheid-era bureaucrat. But we accepted it as a cautionary tale about taking shortcuts with a cat when crossing national borders. We should have known better by now than to neglect the seemingly pointless paperwork.

Most of the Afrikaners I knew would have leapt to rescue Henrietta because she was a *lekker kat.* In Afrikaans, a language that evolved from the original Dutch settlers, *die kat* means "the cat" and the diminutive *katjie,* "a kitten."

The Dutch settlers used the word *kat* as a suffix in naming some of the animals they found in Africa. For instance, *rooikat,* which literally means "red cat," is Afrikaans for a kind of lynx. But *rooikat* is also used to describe a kind of multibarreled handgun that used to be popular with Afrikaners.

And *lekker,* which I understand is of Dutch origin, is one of those all-purpose adjectives meaning "excellent," "enjoyable," or "tasty." *Lekker* was one of a dozen or so words absorbed into our family's vocabulary as we traveled around the world because such words were useful but didn't translate well into English.

Some other words we picked up on our various travels:

Razvorot means "a legal U-turn" in Russian.

Example: "Make a *razvorot,* because we left the cat behind at our last rest stop."

Maalesh, an Arabic word meaning "Don't worry, it doesn't

matter in the least," lacks the sense of urgency conveyed by my poor translation into English.

Example: "*Maalesh,* we can always get around tomorrow to cleaning up the milk the cat spilled if she hasn't licked it up by then."

Meiyou, means, in Chinese, "There isn't any and there wasn't any yesterday, so don't count on there being any tomorrow."

Example: "*Meiyou* cat litter at the Friendship Store on Changan Boulevard."

Meze, a Greek word for a sampling of assorted small, tasty dishes, we picked up on vacations in Greece and Cyprus and thereafter employed to motivate our children to eat leftovers from the refrigerator.

Example: "Feed the cat last night's *meze* before you open a new can for her."

But not until Henrietta went to Johannesburg did I learn to marvel at the linguistic subtleties of African languages. You may smile indulgently when T. S. Eliot in his *Old Possum's Book of Practical Cats* insists that a cat has three names, the third being "his ineffable, effable, efineffable deep and inscrutable singular name," which the poet defines as "the name that no human research can discover—but the cat himself knows, and will never confess."

But the complex Zulu language renders the word "cat" not merely as *ikati,* an approximation of English, but also as *umnangobe,* which according to my Zulu-English dictionary barely scratches the surface. A wild cat is *imbodla* or *incwabe* or *igola.* A civet cat is *insimba.* A witch's cat is *impaka.* And a cat in fables is *inkalimeva.*

This does not begin to cover the idioms and aphorisms in which Zulu oral tradition abounds, nor does it extend to

Henrietta's distant relatives, the bigger cats of Africa. Zulus call a lion an *ingonyama* or *imbube* or *ibhubesi,* depending on the circumstances under which they encounter one; a lioness is *ibhubesi lensikazi.*

This is because well-being, not to mention survival, in Africa depended upon recognizing as many facets of animals as possible, not unlike for the Inuvialuit I knew in northern Canada. In Africa, a cow in the kraal (what we would call a corral) was like money in the bank, a measure of wealth; its meat, milk, and hide were integral to Zulu life. So while a cow is *eyensikazi,* a milking cow is *insengwakazi,* an old cow is *umalukazi,* a cow that just gave birth to a calf is *indlenazi,* and a cow with very little milk is *isigqala.* Zulu offers a valuable truth-in-packaging term—*ulamula*—should someone try to sell you a cow that's a lemon.

In delving into this, I am, as the Zulus say, *nyathelisa okomuntu ophiswe imicabango,* or walking like a cat on hot bricks. But it may explain why, having once fancied myself fluent in Russian and Chinese, I threw up my hands after trying to learn Zulu during my four years in southern Africa.

By the time our *ikati* settled into South Africa, old age was slowing her down. But she showed enough spunk to take on a couple of yapping dogs belonging to our landlady.

South Africa's white suburbs had an abundance of aggressive dogs to scare off poor blacks who appeared at the door asking for work or simply a handout, never mind honest burglars.

When we moved down the street to a new house in suburban Johannesburg, our new landlady greeted us with her antediluvian views about prospects for racial harmony between South Africa's white minority and the black African majority.

"They're barely descended from the trees, you know," she was saying when I heard frantic barking in the kitchen and a responding shriek from Henrietta.

I rushed in to find a couple of her dogs mugging Henrietta, who by now was seventeen years old, a veritable octogenarian calculated in the life expectancy of cats. Who would want to harm a nice little old lady? Teeth bared, they had backed our cat up against the refrigerator and were eager to tear her apart.

But Henrietta wheeled on her assailants as they moved in. Her claws raked the smaller dog across the nose. Spitting and hissing, she lashed out at the larger dog. She was not going down without a fight, even one that she had little chance of winning.

I jumped in, kicked the dogs apart with somewhat more force than necessary, and tried to pick up Henrietta, who looked frail and vulnerable.

She was breathing hard after the fight and would not let me touch her. Her soft gray fur bristled like porcupine quills. Her ears had flattened backward across her small head. Her tail swished violently back and forth.

As soon as Henrietta let me pick her up, I carried her into our new bedroom and shut the door until the landlady departed with her yapping hounds, who were, after all, only indulging the bloodlust encouraged by their owner. I told the landlady what she could do with her dogs.

I felt that Henrietta deserved some medal from the African National Congress for striking back, quite literally, at the running dogs of apartheid.

This is not to say that Henrietta was growing tolerant of other cats. A family down our block later emigrated to England, as quite a few Anglo–South Africans were doing, but were unable to take along their cat, named Peanut Butter, because of the British quarantine. A friend called Jaqueline, who agreed to find Peanut Butter a home.

Henrietta was no more hospitable to the newcomer than she had been to the French doctor's Siamese in Moscow. Howling her outrage at us—"I've given you the best years of my life, and you thank me by bringing in a younger, slimmer trophy cat?"—Henrietta chased Peanut Butter up onto the roof. The next day, Jaqueline, mindful of her promise, took the cat down to Joan, the amiable proprietor of our neighborhood dry cleaning shop. Joan parked Peanut Butter in the shop window, where a customer admired the cat and took him home.

Henrietta had spent her initial months in South Africa chasing warblers and other exquisite small birds around our garden. The region's variety was so profuse that our copy of the *Complete Book of South African Birds* displays colored photographs alone of more than eight hundred indigenous and migratory species.

The last thing Henrietta wanted around was another cat to compete for the tempting variety of migratory fowl. In addition to becoming an expert mouser, she developed a knack for stalking birds after some conspicuous early failures.

In Moscow, she once returned to our apartment through the kitchen window and dropped a sparrow she was carrying between the two windowpanes that insulated us from the winter cold. Jaqueline had a difficult time helping the terrified sparrow fly back into the courtyard before it beat its tiny wings bloody against the opposing glass panes.

But after Henrietta arrived in southern Africa, she changed some of her simplistic assumptions about birds. Her discovery of her inner predator had not allowed for the possibility that she might find herself the prey. Initially, I had qualms about leaving her unattended in our lush garden after hearing horror stories from South Africans about the deaths of pets who had taken on cobras, pit vipers, and mambas, even though these venomous snakes generally inhabited the rural veldt or the semitropical undergrowth around Natal Province.

Henrietta had grown too old to actually catch birds, though she never tired of chasing them. Each time we set out fruit in our backyard to feed the birds, she would emit her huntress growl in anticipation.

Then a flock of hadeda ibises descended on our backyard. They quite liked our garden and showed no intention of sharing it with an American cat by whatever arrangement.

The hadeda takes its name from its harsh call, which sounds like a derisive "ha ha ha de dah." Other African ibises tend toward an admirable reticence in their voice and behavior. The hadeda ibis, however, is loud and obnoxious, the sort of bird that, were it a New Yorker, would quarrel into its cell phone in midconcert or jump in front of you to steal the taxicab you had just hailed after leaving the theater.

The hadeda ibis is not a bird to be intimidated by the likes of an eight-pound cat. These intruders in our garden looked to be about two feet long, with wingspans of three to four feet, and boasted formidably long, curved beaks. Unlike the white fluffy-feathered sacred ibis, which ancient Egyptians revered as the incarnation of learning and wisdom, the red-headed bald ibis, or the improbably long-legged glossy ibis, the hadeda can claim neither beauty nor majesty. The birds that moved in on us ranged from dull gray to dirty khaki in color and emitted squawks at jackhammer decibels that could have been heard by their feathered relations off in Swaziland or Mozambique.

Henrietta, certain that she had the upper paw, was startled to find that the loutish ibises were not only indifferent to her low-throated growl but had decided to chase *her.*

With the hadedas in swift pursuit, flapping their wings and taunting "ha ha ha de dah," Henrietta scampered back to the house and collided several times with the sliding glass door that separated the garden from our living room before finding a narrow opening to one side. Thereafter, she ventured out more gingerly, tail erect and whiskers twitching, looking for cover should the hadedas pursue her again.

Our attempts to chase away the ibises were generally not successful. One got entangled in our clothesline behind the kitchen and resisted Chris's attempts to free it, slapping him with its strong wings and flailing with its long beak. Only eventually did they depart, to Henrietta's relief, though whether they left to mug smaller birds, to carry off young children, or simply to breed more ill-mannered offspring I never figured out.

Our cat also did constant battle with the African ants. Henrietta had chased the occasional ants across our cedar deck in Vermont, but they were nothing like ants in Africa, which are organized enough in some places to erect high-rise anthills out in the bush that stand shoulder-high or taller and are sufficiently solid to withstand blows from anything smaller than a sledgehammer.

Johannesburg had no giant anthills, but it did have subterraneous colonies of semitropical ants that did not take long to detect Henrietta's food bowl through the stucco walls on their over-the-horizon radars.

Jaqueline and I arrived home from a trip to Namibia and noticed a thick, unending black ribbon consisting of countless thousands of ants marching past the outdoor shrubs and under our front door, pivoting with drill-team precision down the hall into our kitchen, and not breaking ranks until they had surrounded and overrun our cat's food.

Some of the ants were swimming in Henrietta's water bowl, splashing one another and having a great old time. It would not have surprised me to learn that they had erected microscopic victory banners and dispatched tiny messengers back to their headquarters announcing "Eureka!" because the effect was the same.

In Vermont, Henrietta had scattered the ants with a swipe of her paw. Such tactics were too meager to succeed in Africa, where she confronted not an ant trickle but an all-out D-Day invasion.

We entered our kitchen to find Henrietta dashing about, trying to beat back the assault on her bowls without success. We picked her up and carried her to the bathroom, where we settled her down with fresh food and water. Then we went back and sprayed the battlefield with whatever unpleasant aerosol we could find, until the invaders lay belly-up or were beating a hasty retreat. It took the rest of the afternoon to scrub the kitchen so the spray wouldn't contaminate Henrietta's food once we brought the bowls back to their old location.

I don't know how our neighbors kept ants away from their pets' feeding bowls, because there weren't that many cats visible around the white suburbs. They tended to live cloistered behind the high gates and walls topped with broken glass and razor wire. But whenever I worked in African townships such as Soweto and Alexandra, I invariably saw cats sunning themselves in front of the shacks and small houses or poking into garbage that the white-run government spent scandalously little money to collect. Here the cats had to work for a living by keeping the rodents at bay, of course, but this made the black townships look definitely cat-friendlier than the white suburbs.

I considered taking Henrietta to see my friends in the townships on one of my next visits. While researching a two-part series about blacks' perceptions of apartheid, Jaqueline and I had spent several days living with a sweet nurse and her friends in the Pimville section of Soweto, and they enjoyed Henrietta when they later came to us for Sunday dinner. But a better opportunity arose to bring the townships, or at least their vitality, to Henrietta.

We had planned not to employ servants in Johannesburg, because the apartheid system, which dictated where people could live and work according to the color of their skin and the texture of their hair, had deliberately created a surfeit of cheap black labor for white exploitation. Such legal constraints—seventeen million Africans were arrested under apartheid for violating laws requiring them to carry passes—gave migrants escaping the grinding poverty of tribal homelands little recourse except to hire out to white employers for the lowest possible wages. But our resolve changed after we met John and Connie Mathatho.

The Mathathos were working as domestics for one of our neighbors in Johannesburg, having left their two small sons back home with relatives in the rural north. White employers usually balked at employing servants who brought along their children, but Connie and John also worried about exposing their boys to the unhealthy seductions of Johannesburg.

John, a hard worker and devout Roman Catholic, turned to us after the neighbor mislaid some plates left from her daughter's first marriage and accused him of taking them. John was innocent, and hurt by this injustice. We suggested that John and Connie move into our house and work a couple of days a week for us while they searched for full-time jobs. We paid them what the African National Congress recommended, which was more than twice the going wage.

Our white neighbors already suspected that we Americans might be gauche enough to pay our staff enough to live on. "Now, don't spoil it for everyone," one matron admonished when I met her returning from the country club in her tennis whites.

We placed an advertisement in the newspapers for the Mathathos, with discouraging results. "What kind of a boy is he, and how much does he want?" one of the callers inquired of John, a dignified man in his thirties who wanted nothing so much as a steady job.

Jaqueline found Connie a job as maid for another woman who would run a finger around the house in search of dust, hoping to find a pretext for not paying Connie what she'd earned. This was not unusual in South Africa, where I interviewed another white employer who supervised her maid by following the terrified woman around with a drawn revolver.

After Connie related her humiliating treatment, Jaqueline paid for her to go to a hairdressing school. Within the year, Connie opened her own small parlor in downtown Johannesburg. Jaqueline later found John, a gifted gardener, a permanent position as groundkeeper for a local primary school.

Connie sometimes helped debone Henrietta's fish and cooked it with peas and beans, which expanded our cat's menu of edible vegetables. Henrietta also found a playmate in the Mathatho's older son, Moses, a shy, serious lad who had an open invitation to come and stay whenever he and his little brother wanted.

When Connie graduated from her course, she and John celebrated by throwing a party for their friends, who were the other maids and gardeners in our neighborhood. Connie planned to hold the party in a nearby park, but I objected. The park was unsafe after dark, and there was a risk that the white policemen who patrolled our neighborhood in a yellow *bakkie,* or pickup truck, might view the party as an illegal gathering of blacks.

"Why not have the party here?" Jaqueline proposed. Connie laughed with delight at this revolutionary notion.

I agreed because it was bound to be fun. I had spent some rollicking evenings drinking Lion beer in the shabeens, the bootleg township taverns, where the men I interviewed always made me feel welcome. Returning the hospitality in some broader way was the least we could do.

Connie and John cooked up plenty of food in our kitchen, and we wrestled our dining-room table out into the garden. Our guests did not arrive until after seven o'clock because they had to wash up after feeding their own employers. They drifted in through our back entrance and insisted upon greeting us with the customary "master" and "madam," which made me wince.

Henrietta ventured forth cautiously to see what was happening. But these visitors had come not with snarling dogs but with rough, callused hands that vied to pet a curious American cat.

We rocked the Johannesburg suburbs on that balmy summer evening. Someone had brought along a boom box and cassette tapes of some terrific Soweto township music. And we danced. I mean, we really danced. I taught Connie a few steps, though maybe it was the other way around. And Jaqueline, who normally sits out anything more casual than a waltz, was jiving to the beat with a dance partner who I'm sure had been mowing grass down the street earlier that afternoon.

Mind you, I'm not saying that Henrietta was dancing too, but even she was finding it hard to sit still through all those syncopated guitar riffs. At the very least, she was rhythmically underfoot.

Abruptly, the music stopped. I checked my watch, and it was barely after nine o'clock. But our guests had quit dancing and set to work cleaning up the garden, which afterward looked a lot tidier than before they had arrived.

"They don't want you to get in trouble with the neighbors," Connie explained.

I was upset to see the party end so soon. Our white neighbors must have been too, because I can't recall that they spoke to us, or Henrietta, after that.

Every farm I visited in South Africa had a few cats to do what farmers around the world expect cats to do. I once flew south to Bloemfontein, a provincial town in the heart of South Africa, to look up Zola Budd Pieterse, the waifish runner whose hope of a gold medal at the 1984 Olympic Games in Los Angeles had been cut short by her collision with an American rival, Mary Decker. With the South Africans returning to the Olympics in 1992, I wanted to know whether Zola, who had run under a British passport in Los Angeles, would compete for her own country this time and what she thought of South Africa's Olympic prospects.

As a track prodigy, Zola Budd Pieterse—she had taken the name of the Afrikaner businessman she had married—was renowned for racing barefoot in international competition. When I met her, she spoke so demurely that her reputation as a flower child seemed undeserved. But having been scalded often by the press, she was understandably nervous about opening up about herself—until I noticed a dappled cat peering at me from under a chair in her living room.

To set Zola at ease, I inquired about her cat and told her about Henrietta's travels. Sensing a sympathetic journalist for a change, Zola shyly confessed that actually she owned three cats.

She also had five dogs, she continued. And eight turkeys and five geese. And fifteen or so chickens. Would I like to meet them?

So we went outside to get acquainted with the rest of her menagerie. One of her turkeys was so handsomely plump that he would make a succulent dinner, and I told her so.

Zola Budd was aghast at my assumption that she was raising her turkeys for the oven. "We don't eat them," she said. "They are my pets."

Like the majority of South Africans, Henrietta lived out her mundane life in the midst of epic times. While I was in Cape Town covering Nelson Mandela's walk to freedom after nearly twenty-eight years in prison, Henrietta marked the historic occasion by catnapping through it. When I later visited Mandela's old prison cell on Robben Island, I wondered whether his long confinement there might have been made more pleasant by the companionship of a cat.

By now, Henrietta's appetite had diminished to the point where she was eating almost nothing. It is not unusual for a cat to go off its food for a while, particularly as the cat gets older and less active.

But one evening, Henrietta did a curious thing that suggested an awareness of imminent mortality. Jaqueline sat on our living-room couch, reading and simultaneously stroking

Henrietta, who had curled up as usual on the adjacent pillow. This time, when Jaqueline stopped petting Henrietta, our cat extended her paw and tapped Jaqueline reprovingly on the arm until the petting resumed.

Again Jaqueline paused to turn a page. And again the supplicatory paw reached forth, beseeching that the display of affection continue. Henrietta continued doing this through the evening, which Jaqueline found curious for a cat with such an independent mind.

In retrospect, it was the natural kind of thing any of us would do to reassure ourselves that we are not forgotten in our old age.

Concerned more about her lethargy and lack of appetite, Jaqueline resolved to take Henrietta to the veterinarian. But then a homeless woman named Sheila, one of the destitute folks living in our local park whom Chris often bought food for, showed up at our door with a broken ankle. I was preparing to leave for Namibia on another reporting trip. Confronted with an emergency, we put our cat's needs out of our thoughts, and Jaqueline drove Sheila to the hospital.

The next day, Henrietta crawled off into the tangled undergrowth behind our house and disappeared.

I searched for a while before I found her hiding under a bush at the far end of our garden. Henrietta did not resist when I put her in my arms and carried her back to the house. Her compact body lacked its familiar weight, sinew, and spirit.

The prospect that she was preparing to die frightened me. It is characteristic of cats to crawl off and meet death in a dignified solitude, rather than be fussed over.

Jaqueline telephoned our veterinarian, and I carried Henrietta out to the car. She did not resist when I placed her in the front seat next to Jaqueline. I had to go back inside and pack for my trip to Namibia.

It was the last time I saw Henrietta.

The veterinarian examined Henrietta and confirmed that she was dying of renal failure. Her kidneys had stopped functioning. Her lungs were slowly filling with fluid. She was finding it difficult to breathe.

"How old is your cat?" the vet asked.

"She's eighteen years," Jaqueline replied.

"Then your cat has lived a long time, hasn't she?" the vet said consolingly. He suggested that Jaqueline take Henrietta home and make her comfortable, and he gave her some medicine to ease the pain. Terribly sorry, he said, but there wasn't anything more that he could do.

He was walking Jaqueline back to our car when Henrietta emitted a shrill shriek. She wriggled out of Jaqueline's arms and jumped. No sooner did she land on the ground than she went limp and lifeless.

Henrietta was dead.

Jaqueline picked up Henrietta and cradled her inert body. The veterinarian asked if my wife wanted to take her home for a few hours anyway. No, Jaqueline replied. But would he please arrange to have Henrietta cremated so that we could take her ashes back for burial among the sugar maples at our house in Vermont? She was, after all, an American cat.

"We usually do a group of animals together," the vet explained. "Cremating your cat separately will cost more."

It had to be a separate cremation, Jaqueline insisted. Henrietta deserved to go home, to really go home.

Jaqueline returned to tell me how Henrietta had died. The next thing she did was to call Celia and Chris, who were both studying back in the United States, and broke the sad news.

My own grief was tinged with disappointment that Henrietta's instinctive reaction in her final moments had been to escape from us, rather than complete her life surrounded by the family who loved her, as you and I would hope to do. But it is pointless to blame animals for failing to imitate human behavior. Henrietta was suffering excruciating pain and responded by trying to flee from it—not from us—hoping to hide out until the pain gave up chasing her and went away.

I did not comprehend this until I read *Catlore,* a study of feline behavior by Desmond Morris, a former curator of animals at the London Zoo. "If we feel sorry for the dying cat that cannot understand what is happening," Mr. Morris wrote, "we should remember that it has one enormous advantage over us. It has no fear of death, something that we humans must all carry with us throughout our long lives."

If a cat does not fear death or cannot understand it, the unawareness of mortality may be a blessing. But must we take this as evidence that a cat has no soul? It is the eschatological sort of question that I am normally content to leave to theologians. Fortunately, our family has one in residence, because Jaqueline earned her Oxford M.A. in theology and was working for an Episcopal church when we met. She tells me that the debate over whether pets have souls remains a lively topic for the letters columns of church newspapers in England.

Incidentally, no such doubts haunt Buddhists, who accept that other living creatures have souls. I've heard that Japanese sometimes hold ceremonies for the souls of their deceased cats.

I know that ecclesiastical dogma in the Western world is

weighted heavily against me, but if cats aren't entitled to souls, why should souls be distributed to the more despicable humans I have covered? I have attended enough wars—from Indochina to the Middle East, Africa, and the Balkans—to have witnessed firsthand mankind's depraved treatment of his fellow man and woman. So pardon me if I express skepticism of the doctrine that all people merit souls while no animal does. I prefer to think of this as one of those mysteries that we see through a glass darkly, as Saint Paul put it to his flock in Corinth. Anyone who adopts a pet can learn something about faith, hope, and love.

For more eloquent testimony, I must yield to Christopher Smart, an eccentric English poet who found himself locked up for madness in a seventeenth-century insane asylum with no one to comfort him but Jeoffry, his cat. As Smart told it, his cat's company was enough to sustain his faith.

"For I will consider my Cat Jeoffry," he wrote. "For he is the servant of the Living God, duly and daily serving him."

Smart's mystical praise of cats is well known, though my favorite verses come from the end of his lengthy poem.

"For he purrs in thankfulness, when God tells him he's a good cat," Smart wrote, following with a summary of Jeoffry's good works that pretty much summarizes what Henrietta brought to our family:

"For he is an instrument for the children to learn benevolence upon.

"For every house is incompleat without him and a blessing is lacking in the spirit . . ."

The last word on souls was spoken in our home in Cairo, when Celia, then twelve years old, was preparing to be confirmed by the local Anglican bishop.

"Does Henrietta have a soul?" Chris asked Celia one day.

"Of course she does," Celia reassured her little brother. "Henrietta has a presoul."

I slept badly the night after Henrietta died. I did not feel like leaving for Namibia the next morning, but I had scheduled too many interviews there to postpone my trip. Jaqueline grieved over Henrietta even more than I did, and I felt miserable about leaving them both behind.

If we had not set Henrietta aside to help Sheila, would it have made any difference? But we are taught to value humans more highly than animals, and in any case, Sheila had had nowhere else to turn; she had lived with us for more than a year. After we left South Africa, Sheila drifted back into homelessness and died on the street.

As my flight descended to the Windhoek airport that brisk morning, I continued to brood about Henrietta, who had passed through the same airport a year or so earlier. I supposed us selfish to have dragged her around the world. Would she have been happier if we had given her away to someone more sedentary, as my parents had done with my pets when we had had to move?

A couple of years earlier, on my first trip to Namibia, the Avis agent at the Windhoek airport had handed over the rental car keys and said almost as an afterthought, "Mind the kudu on the road."

I had no idea what she meant and was too embarrassed to say so. Was "kudu" Afrikaans slang for "potholes"? Or did she mean kudzu, the virulent weed choking the American South? At one point I pulled off the desert road to Windhoek and looked under the car to make sure that I hadn't snagged a kudu, whose leafy tendrils might already be strangling my exhaust pipe.

I didn't sort it out until I set off with a Canadian colleague, Patrick Nagel, across the Namib Desert to Swakopmund, an old German seaside town on Africa's southwestern Atlantic coast.

"Lovely kudu," remarked Pat, who was covering Africa out of Zimbabwe.

I turned and saw a large tan antelope with curved horns and soft eyes intently watch our car approach before bolting into the desiccated brush.

When I recalled the rental agent's enigmatic warning, Pat laughed. Kudu, he explained, often wandered onto a road at night to drink from the puddles of rainwater. Slamming into a kudu was as hazardous as colliding with a moose crossing the highway back in Canada.

Ever after, whenever I rented a car in Namibia, I tried not to smile when I inquired, "Mind the kudu on the road?" This always seemed to impress the rental agent with my knowledge of Africa.

No, I realized, Henrietta could not have thrived in a New York City apartment.

She was born to mind the kudu on the road.

New York

We'd been back in New York for a couple of years when Jaqueline confessed to harboring a secret yen: she wanted another cat. I wasn't immediately aware of her desire, probably because my parents had raised me to behave like a guy, which meant that I wasn't listening.

"No way," I told my sweet wife once the message sank in. "We've already had the world's most lekker cat."

I didn't need some replacement feline, as inferior to the original thing as the temporary spare tire that had come with our Volvo station wagon.

"My mother can't keep up with all three of her cats and offered to let us have one," Jaqueline said as though the prospect had just occurred to her. "Celia thinks that Eliza is the sweetest, so we could try her out for a bit. Will you put down the remote control for a moment and hear me out?"

"What I am hearing," I assured my significant other, "is that we don't need a new cat." Henrietta's ashes must have been swirling around in their tiny ceramic casket in Vermont at the thought of being replaced in our affections.

"You're hardly the quintessential cat lover," Jaqueline observed with her customary astuteness.

"No more cats," I assured her fondly. "One was quite enough." And there the matter seemed to drop.

Anyone reading Henrietta's tale this far could not call me unsympathetic to cats, since my eyes had been opened by the perfect feline specimen, who had shared my bed and board for eighteen years. One man, one cat is the primal compact—or, of course, one woman, one cat. All right, a couple of cats, the exception to this rule being my mother-in-law, who deserves three cats, and for that matter, so does anyone who has ventured this far through my book.

I have met enough celebrity journalists whose smug self-importance might have been ameliorated or corrected altogether by the ownership of a couple of cats, which couldn't care less how much face time you're getting on TV or whether your network ratings soared during sweeps week.

"Of all God's creatures there is only one that cannot be made the slave of the lash," Mark Twain famously observed. "That one is the cat. If man could be crossed with the cat, it would vastly benefit man, but deteriorate the cat."

I was intrigued by a study by Danny Blanchflower, a Dartmouth economist who tried to calculate the cost benefits of happiness. By crunching the numbers, Professor Blanchflower and his colleague Andrew Oswald reckoned that a lasting marriage could yield as much happiness annually as $100,000 in additional income.

Professor Blanchflower has not yet quantified how much a pet is worth, though with four cats, two dogs, two bunnies, and two tree frogs at home, he assured me, "We know their value." So his research may someday enlighten us.

But it might be harder to appraise the value of a pet. How much is your cat worth annually in happiness? Two thousand dollars? Twenty thousand dollars? If so, don't be surprised if you hear shortly from the Internal Revenue Service. But any such estimate would have to become moot when you wake up in those bleak hours after midnight with the next day's worries chewing on your brain, reach over the blanket to touch the warm fur nestled against your side, and hear the soft purr of reassurance that love makes up for a lot in life.

And a cat should know, according to another nineteenth-century contrarian philosopher, Hippolyte Taine, whom you'll know better for his history of English literature, the four volumes of which you may have pretended to have read in their original French to impress your dates in college.

"I have met many thinkers and many cats," Monsieur Taine reported, stroking his mustache pensively, "but the wisdom of cats is infinitely superior."

Still, there can be too much of a good thing, which is to say too many cats per hearth. My best friend, Jack, with whom I toiled as a reporter before he defected to write a couple of best-sellers, earn a real Ph.D., and teach at Dartmouth, rented out his beautiful house in Vermont while he went off to run a postgraduate program.

After a half-dozen years in England, Jack and his wife, Kathy, returned to find their home reeking so thoroughly of cat urine as to be temporarily uninhabitable. In their absence, according to a neighbor, the tenants had lived knee-deep in cats, accumulating as many as thirty of them. I'm not sure whether this estimate includes the carcass of one long-expired cat that the movers uncovered in an upstairs closet or another, live cat that got overlooked in the heating ducts when the tenants moved out.

Jack and Kathy had to rip out the elegant red oak floors, remove the doors and kitchen cabinets, and peel off the bathroom tiles before the really serious scrubbing could begin.

Did you know that all cats in the United States, when they put their bladders to it, manage to collectively pass about nine million gallons of urine a year, much of which sloshed through Jack and Kathy's lovely home? My friends would have done as well renting to Dartmouth fraternity boys, who tend to be as solicitous of other people's property as carpenter ants.

Or Jack and Kathy could have saved some really big bucks by simply leaving their house vacant and flinging open all the windows to let the pipes freeze properly through a half-dozen Vermont winters.

Anyway, one December day in New York, I came home from work, and upon opening our apartment door, I was startled to see—Henrietta?

At first she looked like Henrietta, though as I studied her more closely, the interloper was slightly larger and more brindled, with pronounced tiger striping around the back and tail. Still, the resemblance was uncanny.

It's a wise man, they say, that knows his own cat.

"Say hello to Daddy, Eliza," Jaqueline told her. Eliza obliged by wandering off to recline on our dining-room rug.

"No!" I shouted, enunciating my cri de coeur so clearly that Jaqueline could read my lips without her reading spectacles. "No more cats."

My helpmate was undeterred. "I'm so glad you agree," Jaqueline said, smiling sweetly. "It's just a tryout for a week or two to make sure that you and Eliza like each other. Mother gave her to us and kept her sister, Cleo."

"Can't your mother send this one back to wherever she came from?" I proposed, not realizing that I had bumbled onto a patch of very thin ice.

"I knew you wouldn't want that," Jaqueline said. "Because you remember I told you how Mother found Eliza and Cleo during her vacation in Maine last summer."

"I don't care where she found—" I sputtered.

"Where did she find Eliza and Cleo, you ask?" Jaqueline said, posing the question that I was trying to avoid. "They were in a burlap bag with some stones . . ."

"No more cats," I begged.

" . . . headed for the river," Jaqueline said. "Doesn't Eliza look a little like Henrietta?"

While I pondered their similarity—they would never be mistaken for anything but a couple of cats—Eliza returned to greet me by rubbing against my leg. Her fur felt unusually silky to the touch of my hand.

"Mother thinks she's part Maine coon cat," Jaqueline said. "Maine coon cats have very soft fur, you know."

Jaqueline played her trump card by placing a cup of milk on our breakfast table. What Eliza did next ensured that she would never end up in another sack headed for the Hudson River.

The newcomer hopped up on our breakfast table, but instead of lapping at the milk, Eliza sat down, dipped her left paw into the cup, and daintily raised her paw to her mouth, licking off the milk after each dip.

I was stunned. "Everybody knows that cats don't eat milk with their paw," I said.

Just to prove me wrong, Eliza put her paw into the cup and brought the milk to her mouth again.

Eliza has been eating her milk, and sometimes her dry food, with her paw at our home ever since. How could I turn away a cat who displays better table manners than some of the journalists I know?

Eliza—all thirteen pounds of her, according to her latest visit to the vet—became part of our family. And with that, Jaqueline and I agreed that there would be no more cats.

Some time thereafter, I came home to be greeted by a waifish kitten, smaller and scrawnier than Eliza but with large eyes and an elegantly long, striped tail.

"Say hello to Daddy, Nikki," Jaqueline said.

The kitten sniffed my hand and nipped it.

"What's happened to Eliza?" I demanded.

"Eliza's lonely," my wife said. "She needs someone to keep her company while we're at work."

So Nikki came aboard as Jaqueline's spare cat, presumably in case our prime cat, Eliza, goes on vacation, takes industrial action, or requests a personal day.

Eliza and Nikki spent the first few weeks crouching in front of each other, hissing and boxing and conducting staring marathons, until Nikki got distracted by going into her first heat. Since Nikki returned from being spayed, our Prime Cat and Spare Cat have been taking each other more and more for granted, which is pretty much how they treat me.

Celia, now a magazine editor, and Chris, a newly minted lawyer—who lead their own lives in New York—checked out Jaqueline's choice of cats and expressed approval.

Nikki lies at my elbow as I write this, lolling across the computer keyboard and swatting my fingers with her paw. She inherited from Eliza the responsibility for delaying the completion of my book. Henrietta was professional enough not to interrupt when I was writing on deadline. But Nikki has just been dozing in her freshly cleaned litter box, a curious spot for a catnap, so the grains of clay sticking to her fur drop off one by one between my computer keys. I am wondering where Jaqueline has stored our vacuum cleaner.

Sometimes in setting out supper for Eliza and Nikki at opposite ends of our kitchen, I find myself instinctively calling for Henrietta. I hope the feline ghost that inhabits my memories doesn't mind. I used to wonder how my widowed friends could fall so much in love with a new spouse without forsaking the old partner whose death had rendered them bereft. I hope that I understand better now, however inadequately or imperfectly.

Certainly, our new cats could never diminish my affection for Henrietta, an ordinary cat who thrived on extraordinary adventures.

In the end, we are all solitary, restless creatures. We are not all so gallant.

Acknowledgments

Writing a book about the family cat never figured in my career ambitions as a journalist, so the encouragement of so many friends who cajoled me to just sit down and do it has made all the difference.

Sterling Lord saw the outlines of this book in an article I wrote for the *Times* from Beijing. At Simon & Schuster, Alice Mayhew brought the idea alive and even proposed the title, and her assistant, K. C. Trommer, kept our project deftly on track.

Martin and Marian Goldman, marvelous mentors who taught me that anything worth writing is worth doing well, primed the pump by soliciting my recollections of Henrietta on our walks along the beach at Amagansett, New York.

In the *Times* newsroom, Glenn Collins, Joyce Wadler, Ed Marks, and Claiborne Ray cheered me on while I chipped away at the book in early morning, late evening, and weekends. John Kifner, Steve Weisman, Andy Rosenthal, and Barbara Crossette generously shared their experiences with owning cats abroad.

Jerry Gray, another ex–foreign correspondent who became the best *Times* editor I've worked for, and our mates on the Continuous News Desk tugged me across the finish line.

Among my friends on the *Times* foreign desk, I must thank first Marie Courtney for having been our family's lifeline during our seventeen years overseas. Without Marie's dazzling resourcefulness in surmounting the obstacles we faced moving around the world, we wouldn't have lasted five foreign postings.

Our Vermont neighbors, Chris and Donna Stocking, and Don and Pat Henderson, welcomed Henrietta into their fields and woods during our trips home. Chris's tractor pulled my aging Volvo out of enough ditches in winter to keep my writing from falling hopelessly behind.

I am indebted to the Dana Biomedical Library at Dartmouth Medical School for allowing me access to its books about the physiology and behavior of cats, the better to comprehend these fascinating creatures.

My wife, Jaqueline, now a school librarian, squirreled away so many books during our time abroad that when I looked at how other writers considered cats, I found not one but two copies of Thoreau's *Walden,* Chekhov's short stories in both Russian and English, and three poetry anthologies containing Christopher Smart's praise of his cat Jeoffry.

Jaqueline undertook archeological digs into the unpacked boxes filling our basement in Vermont and unearthed photographs, letters, and children's writings about Henrietta's life abroad.

This book was very much a family effort. Our daughter, Celia, set aside her deadline responsibilities as managing editor of *American Theater* magazine to tighten up my manuscript and propose changes and corrections that were pitch-perfect.

And our son, Chris, found time in his 168-hour work weeks as a new lawyer for Hogan and Hartson to summon up anecdotes and other insights about Henrietta that I had quite forgotten.

For Henrietta and for me, they have been the greatest blessing.

about the author

Christopher S. Wren, a reporter and editor for *The New York Times,* has served as its bureau chief in Moscow, Beijing, Cairo, Ottawa, and Johannesburg and as its correspondent at the United Nations. He has also covered New York City and national stories for the newspaper. His book *The End of the Line: The Failure of Communism in the Soviet Union and China* was designated a notable book of 1990 by *The New York Times Book Review.* His novel about foreign correspondents, *Hacks,* was published in 1996.